Vincent Schade

The inclusion of aviation in the European Emission Trading Scheme

Analyzing the scope of impact on the aviation industry

Anchor Academic
Publishing

Schade, Vincent: The inclusion of aviation in the European Emission Trading Scheme: Analyzing the scope of impact on the aviation industry. Hamburg, Anchor Academic Publishing 2013

Buch-ISBN: 978-3-95489-189-4
PDF-eBook-ISBN: 978-3-95489-689-9
Druck/Herstellung: Anchor Academic Publishing, Hamburg, 2013

Bibliografische Information der Deutschen Nationalbibliothek:
Die Deutsche Nationalbibliothek verzeichnet diese Publikation in der Deutschen Nationalbibliografie; detaillierte bibliografische Daten sind im Internet über http://dnb.d-nb.de abrufbar.

Bibliographical Information of the German National Library:
The German National Library lists this publication in the German National Bibliography. Detailed bibliographic data can be found at: http://dnb.d-nb.de

Vincent Schade

The inclusion of aviation in the European Emission Trading Scheme

Analyzing the scope of impact on the aviation industry

Anchor Academic
Publishing

Schade, Vincent: The inclusion of aviation in the European Emission Trading Scheme: Analyzing the scope of impact on the aviation industry. Hamburg, Anchor Academic Publishing 2013

Buch-ISBN: 978-3-95489-189-4
PDF-eBook-ISBN: 978-3-95489-689-9
Druck/Herstellung: Anchor Academic Publishing, Hamburg, 2013

Bibliografische Information der Deutschen Nationalbibliothek:
Die Deutsche Nationalbibliothek verzeichnet diese Publikation in der Deutschen Nationalbibliografie; detaillierte bibliografische Daten sind im Internet über http://dnb.d-nb.de abrufbar.

Bibliographical Information of the German National Library:
The German National Library lists this publication in the German National Bibliography. Detailed bibliographic data can be found at: http://dnb.d-nb.de

I Table of Contents

II Table of Figures

III List of Abbreviations

AAU/s	Assigned Amount Unit/s
A-CDM	Airport Collaborative Decision Making
art.	Article
ATC	Air Traffic Control
ATK/s	Available Ton Kilometer/s
ATM	Air Traffic Management
CDM	Clean Development Mechanism
CER/s	Certified Emission Reduction/s
CO_2	Carbon dioxide
EC	European Commission
EEA	European Economic Area
EEX	European Energy Exchange
ERU/s	Emission Reduction Unit/s
ETS/s	Emission Trading Scheme/s
EU	European Union
EUA/s	European Emission Allowance/s
EU-ETS	European Union Emission Trading Scheme
GHG/s	Greenhouse gas/es
IATA	International Air Transport Association
ICAO	International Civil Aviation Organization
IET	International Emission Trading
IPCC	Intergovernmental Panel on Climate Change
JI	Joint Implementation
KP	Kyoto Protocol

LCC/s	Low-cost carrier/s
NAP/s	National Allocation Plan/s
NWC/s	Network carrier/s
par.	Paragraph
R&D	Research and development
RTK/s	Revenue Ton Kilometer/s
SESAR	Single European Sky ATM Research
UN	United Nations
UNFCCC	United Nations Framework Convention on Climate Change

1 Introduction

1.1 Background

Climate change has been a major concern in climate policy and has therefore regularly been on politicians agenda for a long time. For this reason, several scientific studies in climate research were conducted to detect main causes of this disturbing environmental development. It was determined that anthropogenic (i.e., human-induced) greenhouse gases (GHGs), such as nitrous oxide (N_2O), methane (CH_4), and carbon dioxide (CO_2), have been major contributors of global warming.[1] In particular, atmospheric CO_2 concentration, which is caused by the combustion of carbon based fuels, has been declared as one of the major drivers of the greenhouse effect. Beyond that, records show a significant increase of atmospheric CO_2 concentration compared to pre-industrial levels.[2] In order to address these climate change challenges and mitigate global warming, international environmental treaties, such as the United Nations Framework Convention on Climate Change (UNFCCC) and later the Kyoto Protocol (KP), were established to enforce limitations on GHG emissions.[3] As a result, the overall GHG emissions within the European Union (EU) were decreased by 5.5% between 1993 and 2003.[4] Moreover, additional actions were taken through the creation of the European Union Emission Trading Scheme (EU-ETS) in 2003. This cap-and-trade scheme operates through the allocation and trade of emission allowances to reduce GHG emissions in a cost effective manner. Its original scope required only selected industries, such as energy, iron, and oil, to comply with the emission trading scheme (ETS).[5] Aviation, as an industry whose CO_2 emissions have risen in the EU by 95% since 1990, accounts nowadays for about 3.3% of the EU's total CO_2 emissions. However, it had never been subject to the KP nor included in the EU-ETS.[6] In 2008, the European Commission (EC) proposed the inclusion of aviation in the EU-ETS as a response to the continuous air traffic growth which caused a constant increase of CO_2 emissions from aviation. As a result, Directive

[1] See Grubb (2003), p. 147.
[2] See Intergovernmental Panel on Climate Change (2007); Kiehl and Trenberth (1997).
[3] See United Nations (1992); United Nations (1997).
[4] See Wit et al. (2005), p. 1.
[5] See European Commission (2003), Annex I.
[6] See European Environment Agency (2012), pp. 293-294.

2008/101/EC (henceforth Aviation Directive), an amendment of the original EU-ETS legislation, was ratified and came into force in January 2012. Since then, all flights departing from and arriving at an airport located in the European Economic Area (EEA) have been subject to the EU-ETS.[7] Figure 1 illustrates the long-term evolution of global air traffic between 1980 and 2007, including major events leading to some temporary variations of activity:

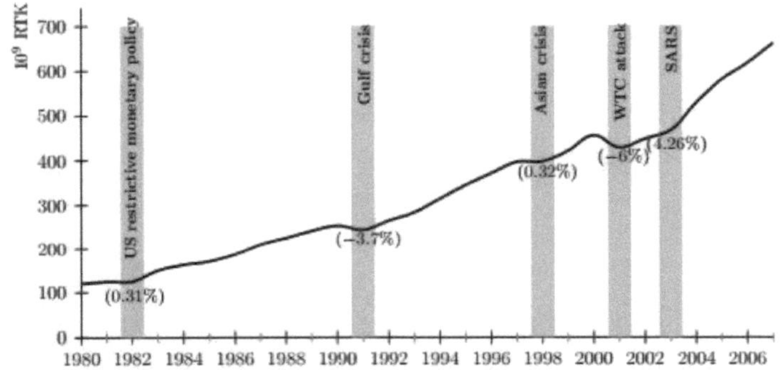

Figure 1: Evolution of world air traffic (1980-2007) expressed in RTK (billions)[8]

A significant volume of literature already exists concerning the inclusion of aviation in the EU-ETS. Most of the research laid its focus on specific industry levels such as the individual airline, the aviation industry in general or macroeconomic aspects. In this context, these studies tried to anticipate market reactions triggered by the EU-ETS by analyzing specific issues such as the financial impact on airlines, changes in competitive behavior or implications for the overall industry development.[9] As a consequence, the existing studies took only a limited market view and made assumptions about expected developments in specific fields of the aviation industry. However, at the time of writing this thesis, conclusions about the scope of impact could hardly be drawn from existing impact assessments because of the wide range of issues that exceeded the scope of most impact studies. Hence, a broader research approach is needed which takes

[7] See European Commission (2008), preamble, par. 16; The EEA consists of the EU, Iceland, Liechtenstein, and Norway.
[8] See Chèze et al. (2011), p. 5.
[9] See Anger (2010); Lowe et al. (2007); Scheelhaase and Grimme (2007).

different analytical perspectives to describe the scope of impact of the EU-ETS and depict potential effects for the aviation industry.

1.2 Objective and limitations

The main objective of this thesis is to describe the scope of impact of the EU-ETS on aviation and to develop a detailed understanding of the effects for the aviation industry through its inclusion in the EU-ETS.

Facilitated by the following remarks, including a comprehensive impact analysis, this thesis will also help to understand:

- the potential chances and risks for airlines through the recent incorporation in the EU-ETS,
- the expected market development of the aviation industry in the future due to the imposition of an ETS for GHG emissions,
- the international legal framework for climate change and emission trading, and
- the distinct industry characteristics, including interrelations and dependencies between the legislation and the aviation industry.

Due to the complexity of the research topic, the presented analysis in this thesis is conducted under scope limitations. The focus of the analysis is to examine the impact of the EU-ETS on passenger airlines, excluding cargo airlines and other market participants such as airport operators, ground handlers or other service providers.[10] Also, adjacent industries such as tourism and the oil industry are not subjects of the analysis.

1.3 Structure

This master thesis is structured into six main sections. After the introduction, section two provides the reader with an overview of the legal framework for climate policy in order to describe the legal scope of major climate policy treaties and explain how the EU-ETS is embedded in this legal environment. At first, international and national law is conceptualized by distinguishing between different environmental treaties. Later remarks refer to

[10] In this thesis, the terms "aviation industry" and "airline industry" are used interchangeably.

major climate change treaties such as the UNFCCC and the KP. Eventually, a detailed description of the EU-ETS, including its objectives, scope, and mechanisms, is given. Based on the preceding part, section three delves further into the EU-ETS by focusing on the aviation industry and its incorporation in the EU-ETS. In the beginning, a brief overview of key characteristics of the aviation industry is provided to achieve a sufficient understanding of the market players, the competitive situation, and major industry trends. Subsequently, the section elaborates on environmental policies in international aviation ending with a detailed description of the Aviation Directive including its objectives, design parameters, and latest amendments. Section four encompasses a comprehensive analysis of EU-ETS describing the scope of impact for the aviation industry. Different industry parameters that are potentially impacted through the inclusion in the EU-ETS are identified. Moreover, expected effects for the industry are highlighted and potential market reactions of airlines are discussed to provide support for future predictions on industry developments. In order to achieve an overall understanding of the scope of impact, the impact assessment takes three distinct analysis perspectives. The individual perspective focuses on the impact of the EU-ETS on airline profitability. Subsequently, the intra-industry perspective takes a broader view on the impact on competition between market players. Eventually, the collective industry perspective focuses on potential changes in market performance and development, and thereby examines effects for the overall aviation industry. Thereafter, section five outlines main results from the impact analysis, including main drivers of impact for aviation. Later, management implications for airlines to cope with the EU-ETS regulatory are discussed. Finally, section six concludes this thesis by recapitulating the key aspects of the research topic and providing a future outlook for potential developments regarding the EU-ETS and the aviation industry.

2 Legal framework for climate change and emission trading

2.1 Demarcation of international and EU law for climate change

In order to understand the legal framework for climate change and the embeddedness of the EU-ETS in this system, it is important to differentiate between international and EU treaties. Furthermore, it helps to clarify the legal scope of the respective treaties at the international and EU level.

The UNFCCC is an international environmental convention on climate change. It was negotiated at the United Nations Conference on Environment and Development in 1992 and has been effective since March 1994.[11] At that time, GHGs were declared as a major driver of climate change which raised the awareness of the fact that human-induced emissions cause global warming. However, the UNFCCC did not contain any legal obligations for climate change prevention. Instead, as a multilateral environmental convention it provided the framework for negotiations about further, more specific, multilateral agreements to protect the climate system.[12]

In later years, the UN adopted the KP, which has become the most prominent treaty established under the umbrella of the UNFCCC. As a multilateral treaty against climate change, it specifies the original objectives of the UNFCCC and sets legally binding and quantified emission targets. As to date, the UNFCCC has been ratified by 195 parties, including major economies such as the EU and the United States of America (USA).[13] Article (art.) 4 of the KP entitles the EU member states to fulfill their KP emission targets collectively.[14] Under this rule, which is often called the "EU Bubble", the EU takes on a distinct role under the KP legislation since it allows for regional legal enforcements of emission mitigation measures within the community.

As a result, the EU-ETS was launched as part of the European Climate Change Program in October 2003. With the introduction of the EU-ETS, the EU decided to jointly

[11] See United Nations Framework Convention on Climate Change (2013); United Nations (1992), art. 23 (1).
[12] See United Nations (1992).
[13] See United Nations Framework on Climate Change (2012b); In addition to each EU member state, the EU signed the KP collectively as a community of states; The last ratifying country was Andorra on 2 March 2011.
[14] See United Nations (1997), art. 4.

fulfill the Kyoto targets, and thereby achieving its own environmental targets.[15] Figure 2 depicts the previously described treaties and their inclusion within the legal framework of climate policy:

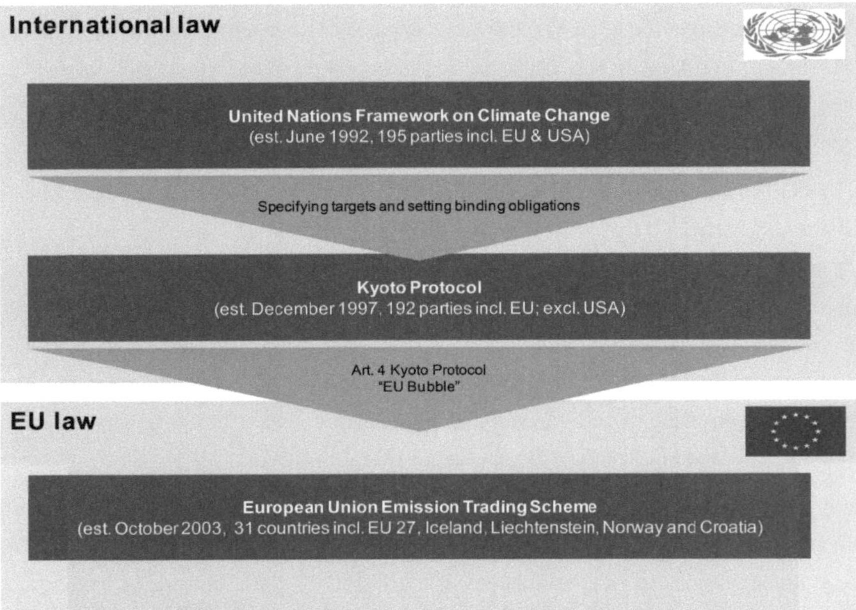

Figure 2: Legal framework for climate policy[16]

2.2 United Nations Framework Convention on Climate Change

The ultimate objective of the UNFCCC is the "stabilization of greenhouse gas concentrations in the atmosphere at a level that would prevent dangerous anthropogenic interference with the climate system".[17] To achieve its objective, the UNFCCC demands from its parties to reduce their GHG emissions without setting legally binding quantified limitations on GHG emission levels.[18] In order to account for the varying development stages and economical capabilities of the convention parties, the UNFCCC differentiates

[15] See European Commission (2003), preamble, par. 5.
[16] Own illustration.
[17] See United Nations (1992), art. 2.
[18] See United Nations (1992), art. 4 (2).

between developed (Annex I parties) and developing countries (non-Annex parties) regarding expected initiatives to combat climate change.[19] Furthermore, the UNFCCC explicitly states to ensure equity between its parties and therefore applies "the principal of common but differentiated responsibilities" which imposes all parties to protect the climate system; however, developed countries ought to take the lead in implementing precautionary measures against climate change. Also, industrialized nations are required to support developing countries that bear a disproportional burden under the UNFCCC.[20]

2.3 Kyoto Protocol

The KP is an international environmental agreement based on the UNFCCC which specifies the objective of preventing climate change by setting quantitative limitations on GHG emissions.[21] Although the KP was originally adopted in December 1997, it did not enter into force until February 2005 because of the USA's withdrawal from the protocol in 2000. In order to become effective, art. 25 KP requires the signing of not less than 55 countries, whose overall CO_2 emissions total at least 55% of the global CO_2 emissions for 1990.[22] Since the USA withdrew from the protocol in 2000, the remaining KP parties had not fulfilled this requirement until Russia's ratification in late 2004. Since then, 192 parties have been obliged to comply with the Kyoto emission targets.[23] The KP follows a sequential timeline consisting of distinct commitment periods for which specific emission targets are set. The first commitment period ran from 2008 to 2012 whereas the second commitment period will span from 2013 to 2020 as recently decided at the UN Climate Change Conference in Doha. However, amendments concerning emission targets made on this conference are yet to be approved by the parties.[24] For the first period, it was agreed to reduce overall GHG emissions by at least 5% compared to the base year.[25]

[19] Annex I parties are developed countries and countries that are undergoing the process of transition to a market economy. Non-annex countries include all developing countries that have signed and ratified the KP.
[20] See United Nations (1992), art. 3.
[21] GHGs covered by the KP include CO_2, CH_4, N_2O, HFC_s, PFC_s and SF_6.
[22] See United Nations (1997), art. 25; Freestone (2005), p. 9.
[23] See United Nations Framework on Climate Change (2012a); United Nations Climate Change Secretariat (2004).
[24] See United Nations Framework on Climate Change (2012c).
[25] See United Nations (1997), art. 3 (1); The base year for most parties is 1990 except Bulgaria (1988),

During these negotiations the EU was committed to a mutual emission reduction target of 8% which is known as the Burden Sharing Agreement.[26]

Similar to the UNFCCC, the KP also acknowledges the different industrialized levels of its parties and therefore only requires developed nations listed in Annex I of the UNFCCC to comply with its quantified emission targets.[27] In order to regulate emission levels, each Annex I party initially obtains so called Assigned Amount Units (AAUs) which are calculated by applying the party's emission reduction target to the GHG emissions in the base year.[28] If a KP party fails to meet the predetermined reduction targets, a penalty of 30% for each excess emission unit (hereinafter Kyoto unit) is enforced. This means that for each ton of GHG emissions, which exceeds the reduction target, 1.3 Kyoto units will be deducted from its AAUs for the subsequent commitment period.[29] In order to increase the flexibility of the KP and increase cost efficiency to meet reduction targets, KP parties are allowed to add or subtract Kyoto units from their AAUs through the use of flexible mechanisms.[30] The KP provides three flexible mechanisms which are widely known as Kyoto mechanisms. These are, Joint Implementation (JI), the Clean Development Mechanism (CDM), and International Emission Trading (IET).[31]

JI is a project-based mechanism in which an Annex I party invests in an emission reduction project in another Annex I party.[32] As a result, the investing party receives Emission Reduction Units (ERUs) in addition to its AAUs while deducting the same amount of Kyoto units from the beneficiary's account. In this way, the total amount of Kyoto units does not increase but Kyoto units are only redistributed.[33]

The CDM constitutes another project-based mechanism which enables KP parties to acquire additional Kyoto units. In contrast to JI projects, a CDM rewards Annex I parties after investing in emission reduction projects conducted in developing countries.[34] In

---

Hungary (average of 1985-1987), Poland (1988), Romania (1989), and Slovenia (1986).

[26] See European Council (2002a).

[27] See United Nations (1997), art. 3 (1).

[28] See United Nations (1997), art. 3 (7).

[29] See United Nations Framework on Climate Change (2008), p. 29.

[30] See United Nations (1997), art. 3 (10-12).

[31] Further EUAs can be acquired through land use, land use change, and forestry activities (LULUCF) which are not discussed in this thesis due to its low significance for the aviation industry.

[32] See United Nations (1997), art. 6.

[33] See United Nations Framework on Climate Change (2008), p. 17.

[34] See United Nations (1997), art. 12.

those projects, the funding party receives so called Certified Emission Reductions (CERs) which can be converted into Kyoto units. Since emissions from non-Annex parties are not subject to the KP, CDM projects increase the total amount of Kyoto units, and thereby allow for increased GHG emissions under the KP.[35]

Unlike the preceding Kyoto mechanism, IET represents a market-based mechanism which creates the framework for international trade of Kyoto units between the KP parties.[36] The IET gives KP parties, whose projected GHG emissions exceed the AAUs, the opportunity to acquire additional Kyoto units through trading activities on the carbon market. In turn, it enables KP parties, whose GHG emissions are lower than their AAUs, to gain profits through the sale of unused Kyoto units to high-emitting parties. Moreover, the trading opportunity of unused Kyoto units encourages KP parties to take domestic actions, and thereby reduce GHG emissions. To prevent future compliance issues with emission targets resulting from intensive trading of Kyoto units, KP parties are obliged to retain a certain number of Kyoto units to maintain a so called commitment period reserve.[37] However, the IET does not prescribe any domestic or regional ETSs it rather constitutes the foundation on which other ETS can be established. Yet, all trading activities carried out under sub-ETSs are subject to the KP and need to comply with the KP emission targets.[38] In the following, the EU-ETS as the most prominent regional sub-ETS of the KP is described.

2.4 European Union Emission Trading Scheme

2.4.1 Motivation and objectives

The EU had always been an advocate for the battle against climate change. Accordingly, the EU urged to take policy measures to prevent global warming. It was predicted that an increase of the global annual mean surface temperature by more than 2°C above pre-industrial levels would cause irreversible catastrophic events.[39] Also, it was obvious

[35] See United Nations Framework on Climate Change (2008), p. 18.

[36] See United Nations Framework on Climate Change (2012d); United Nations (1997), art.17; ERUs and CERs obtained through emission reduction projects are tradable emission units on the carbon market.

[37] See United Nations Framework on Climate Change (2008), p. 58.

[38] See United Nations Framework on Climate Change (2008), p. 16.

[39] See European Commission (2005).

that the 8% decrease in CO_2 emissions confirmed under the Burden Sharing Agreement would not be sufficient to achieve this target. Scientific findings by the Intergovernmental Panel on Climate Change (IPCC) had indicated that a sustainable global CO_2 emission reduction of at least 50% below 1990 levels must be achieved by 2050 to avoid severe climate change events.[40] For this reason, additional mitigation measures were needed to further curtail CO_2 emissions. This led to the creation of the EU-ETS in October 2003. Since its launch in January 2005, it has been a cornerstone of European climate policy and presents the central instrument of the EU Climate and Energy Package from December 2008. Under this initiative, the EU pursues a 20% GHG emission reduction compared to 1990 emission levels by the year 2020.[41]

2.4.2 Scope and extensions

As to date, the EU-ETS has been introduced in 31 countries including the 27 EU member states as well as neighboring countries such as Norway, Liechtenstein, Iceland, and Croatia. As an entity-based ETS, the EU-ETS covers some 11,000 installations across several high-emitting industries, including energy, oil, coke, metal ore, and steel.[42] In its entirety the EU-ETS accounts for around half of the CO_2 emissions released in the EU.[43] This makes the EU-ETS the largest multinational ETS against climate change.[44]

Since its launch, the EU-ETS has experienced several scope extensions as for instance the incorporation of N_2O which results from the production of nitric acid.[45] Also, extensions of the legal scope to non-EU countries such as Iceland, Liechtenstein, and Norway were accomplished.[46] In addition, the international civil aviation industry, as the first segment of the transportation industry, was incorporated by adopting the Aviation Directive. Besides sectoral and GHG-specific extension plans, the EU pursues further geographical scope extension by promoting the EU-ETS beyond community borders. This also emphasizes the EU's overall vision of developing an international network of

---

[40] See Intergovernmental Panel on Climate Change (2007).
[41] See European Council (2008).
[42] Within an entity-based ETS emission allowances are traded between companies.
[43] See European Commission (2013a).
[44] See European Commission (2009b), p. 5.
[45] See European Commission (2009b), p. 13.
[46] Croatia joined the EU-ETS in January 2013 leading to 31 member states covered by the EU-ETS.

ETSs and creating a global carbon market.[47] Art. 25 of the EU-ETS explicitly states the openness to other compatible mandatory GHG ETSs. In this regard, officials from the EU and the Australian government recently reached an agreement on linking the schemes by 2018.[48]

2.4.3 Allocation and cap system

The EU-ETS operates as a cap-and-trade scheme. This means that it sets a limit on the total amount of GHGs that are allowed to be released by the members under the scheme.[49] The cap determines the total amount of emission allowances, so called EU Emission Allowances (EUAs), which the members receive to cover their emissions. If emissions from business operations exceed the amount of EUAs, members need to engage in trading activities to buy or sell EUAs on the carbon market. Also, as a sub-trading system of the KP, the EU-ETS entitles members to use Kyoto credits to cover emissions as agreed under the Linking Directive.[50]

EUAs are allocated using a combination of auctioning and free allocation whereas the majority of EUAs are allocated free of cost by applying a benchmarking scheme. The quantity of EUAs that are freely allocated depends on the specific industry and its competitive situation on the global market to ensure competitiveness of the European economy. However, in order to achieve the ambitious emission reduction targets and generate revenues for EU mitigation measures, the EU intends to steadily increase the share of EUAs allocated under auctioning.[51] The free allocation of EUAs to stationary installations, such as industrial plants, follows a product benchmark. This benchmark represents the 10% most efficient installations whose performance is compared to eligible installations to determine the number of free EUAs allocated to the members.[52] At the end of every year, each member must surrender EUAs equivalent to the respec-

---

[47] See European Commission (2003), art. 25.
[48] See European Commission (2013e).
[49] See European Commission (2013a).
[50] See European Commission (2004).
[51] See European Commission (2013a).
[52] See European Commission (2011a).

tive emission level of the year. If emissions exceed the quantity of EUAs, financial penalties are imposed by the regulatory authorities of the member states.[53]

2.4.4 Trading and price mechanisms

As mentioned earlier, the EU-ETS is an entity-based ETS. As such, individual companies perform emission trading on a common carbon market.[54] On the contrary, IET under the KP solely takes place between KP parties at a national level.[55] It should be noted that emission trading refers to the trade of emission rights as opposed to trading of emissions themselves. In this context, an emission right is the permission to release a certain amount of CO_2 within a specific period of time.[56] Besides trading with EUAs, the EU decided to link the Kyoto project-based mechanisms to the EU-ETS. Since then, EU-ETS members are allowed to use a limited number of Kyoto credits to cover emissions under the EU-ETS and trade international credits (JI and CDM) on the carbon market.[57] Beyond the general trade of EUAs, the EU-ETS legislation allows for inter-temporal trading which involves banking and borrowing of EUAs. Banking enables EU-ETS members to carry EUAs to future years whereas borrowing describes the use of future emission allowances to cover emissions from current operations. The inter-temporal trade gives members more flexibility to use EUAs under dynamic emission levels. However, to avoid compliance issues in future periods, the EU-ETS does not allow inter-period borrowing across compliance periods.[58] In order to achieve emission reductions and stimulate emission mitigation actions, the EU imposes an emission cap based on historical emission levels which are lower than emissions released under current economic activities. This results in EUA scarcity and creates value for the emission allowances so that a market price can be established.[59] Also emitters are encouraged to manage business operations more effectively and lower carbon emissions in order to ease the cost burden of emission charges.

---

[53] See European Commission (2003), art. 16.
[54] In the following the terms "companies" and "members" are used interchangeably.
[55] See United Nations (1997), art. 3, 17.
[56] See De Witt Wijnen (2005), p. 403; European Commission (2003), art. 3; Under the EU-ETS, an EUA represents the right to emit one metric ton of CO_2 within a given year.
[57] See European Commission (2004); For further details see also: Jepma (2003).
[58] See Chevallier (2012), pp. 157-158.
[59] See Faber and Brinke (2011), p. 3.

2.4.5 Timeline and structural changes

The EU-ETS is periodically divided into consecutive trading phases. The first trading phase commenced in 2005 and spun over three years ending in 2007. It is often called the trial period as it was primarily pursued to gain experience in the operation of a multinational ETS, to establish an effective carbon price, and to provide seamless free trade of EUAs across the EU. Simultaneously, the implementation of a functioning infrastructure to perform reliable monitoring, reporting, and verification of emission data was a main objectives during the initial phase. Hence, significant CO_2 emission reductions were not expected during this time period.[60] Phase two ran from 2008 to 2012 coinciding with the first Kyoto commitment period. During this period, various changes of the community scheme were made to solve teething problems and ensure a more effective ETS against climate change. In this regard, allocation rules were changed, geographical scope extensions were conducted, and the Kyoto mechanisms were linked to the community scheme.[61] As it can be seen, the EU-ETS as the largest multinational ETS requires constant revision by the policymakers to maintain an effective instrument against climate change. Especially, the size and complexity of the scheme has caused problems to implement a resilient scheme which does not require continuous modifications to achieve its objectives. Since its introduction, the EU-ETS has required various structural changes to improve its effectiveness and achieve its environmental goals. The EU-ETS has recently ended its second trading period. The EC proposes further structural changes for the current period which runs from 2013 to 2020. In the following, current developments regarding structural reforms of the EU-ETS are addressed.

In order to increase transparency and lower the complexity of several autonomous National Allocation Plans (NAPs), the EC decided to introduce a harmonized allocation methodology at EU level. Since 2013, EUAs have been centrally allocated applying a community-wide emission cap. This initiative promises to prevent member states from applying discriminatory measures, as they will no longer be able to favor their national industries under the NAPs.[62] Moreover, the third period will experience a significant shift from free allocation to auctioning. In this regard, it is proposed to assign at least 50% of

[60] See Elleman and Joskow (2008), p. iii.
[61] See European Commission (2013b).
[62] See European Commission (2011a).

all EUAs through auctioning. In addition, a more stringent cap will be enforced which will decrease annually by 1.74%, reaching a 21% emission decrease compared to 2005 levels at the end of the period.[63]

To raise environmental awareness outside the EEA and increase the international reach of its ETS, the EU has promoted the EU-ETS outside the EEA and has tried to establish links to other national or regional ETSs. As a first step towards a global network of carbon ETSs, officials from the EU and Australia recently announced to link their ETSs. Both countries agreed on establishing a full link between the two systems by 1 July 2018. This means that the free trade of emission allowances between Australian and European businesses will be possible. In addition, there are ongoing negotiations about linking the EU-ETS with the Swiss ETS. The merger of ETSs can potentially decrease system costs, increase market liquidity, and create a more stable carbon market.[64]

There are currently debates about measures to ensure price stability on the carbon market. During the first and second trading period there have been system flaws that led to critical price falls on the carbon market. For instance, the former high level of decentralization made individual member states responsible to allocate EUAs to their national businesses. Under NAPs, large companies lobbied for a fair allocation of EUAs to prevent disadvantages in global competition. As a result, EUAs were distributed too generously at the national level which led to an oversupply of EUAs within the EU.[65] In addition, companies were not allowed to bank excess EUAs for further use in future trading periods.[66] As a consequence, the carbon price plummeted sharply in May 2006 reaching its low in 2007 at almost 0€/t CO_2. The price recovered at the beginning of phase two, reaching its peak in August 2008 at 28€/t CO_2 before falling again shortly after.[67] This price collapse was predominantly indebted by the economic downturn during this period which led to a decline in demand for EUAs. Since mid 2009, the EUA price had been fairly stable at around 15 €/t CO_2 before dropping again below 10 €/t in the second half of 2011 as outlined in figure 3:

[63] See European Commission (2009b), p. 12.
[64] See European Commission (2013c).
[65] See Egenhofer et al. (2011), p. ii.
[66] See European Commission (2003), art. 13.
[67] See European Energy Exchange (2013a).

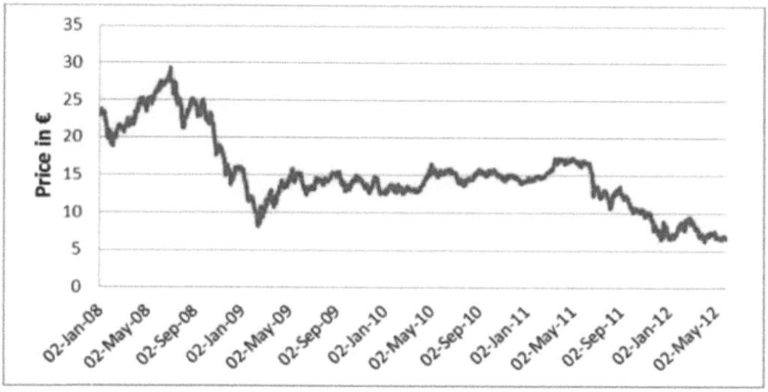

Figure 3: Carbon price evolution (data for front-year futures contracts with delivery in December)[68]

As a result from a slowing economy over previous years, companies were able to build up a huge surplus of EUAs which was projected to reach some 1.5 to 2 billion EUAs in 2013.[69] In order to prevent a repeated price fall and ease the impact of the EUA surplus on demand for emission allowances, the EC set out a range of measures to stabilize the carbon market. First, the EC refrained from the allocation of EUAs under NAPs and implemented a centralized EUA allocation at the EU level to prevent a further over-allocation of EUAs.[70] Moreover, the EC plans to back-load some 900 million EUAs for the third trading period. This implies a deferral of EUA allocation to the end of the trading period. In this way, the current EUA surplus is expected to gradually decrease and EUAs are more evenly distributed over the individual years of the trading period.[71] Furthermore, in a recent report the EC proposes the following measures to sustain an effective supply and demand relation and regain price stability in the carbon market:

- increasing the EU reduction target to 30% in 2020,
- retiring a number of EUAs in phase three permanently,
- revising the current annual linear reduction factor of 1.74% before 2020,
- extending the scope of the EU-ETS to other sectors,
- limiting the access to Kyoto credits, and

[68] See European Commission (2012b), p. 5.
[69] See European Commission (2013d).
[70] See European Commission (2011a).
[71] See European Commission (2012a).

- establishing discretionary price management mechanisms such as a carbon price floor or an allowance reserve.[72]

However, each of these proposed measures are still under debate and have yet to be passed by the EU legislative in order to be enforced.

[72] See European Commission (2012b).

3 International aviation and climate change

3.1 International aviation industry and airline economics

In order to understand the implications of emission charges for airlines, it is important to have general knowledge about specific characteristics of the aviation industry. This also helps to comprehend distorting effects on different airlines and to make projections for future industry developments. The following remarks highlight industry-specific parameters describing the overall industry, including the past evolution, current competitive situation, market players, and major industry trends, to provide relevant information for the later impact analysis.

3.1.1 Market evolution and competition

The aviation industry has experienced a dynamic development for a long time. In particular, several liberalization and deregulation measures have turned the aviation market from a formerly highly regulated industry into a truly globalized market. The Airline Deregulation Act which was passed by the US congress in 1978 is frequently mentioned as a pioneer for deregulation which triggered a move towards an open aviation market. The treaty phased out governmental regulations over air fares, flight routes, and barriers to enter the US aviation market for foreign airlines.[73] Following this trend, similar efforts were made throughout the world, e.g. in Canada (1984), New Zealand (1986), Australia (1990) and Europe (1992-1997).[74]

The deregulation instigated a reorganization and strategic realignment of airline business models which was supposed to meet global industry demand more effectively. As a result, the renowned hub-and-spoke system became widely the preferred network configuration since it enabled airlines to increase aircraft utilization while providing a larger route network for passengers.[75] In contrast to the widespread hub-and-spoke model, Southwest Airlines has been a prominent exemption by following its low-cost strategy since its foundation in 1967. Today, Southwest Airlines is seen as the pioneer

---

[73] See United States Congress (1978).
[74] See Gillen (2006), p. 367.
[75] See Gillen (2006), p. 368.

of the low-cost business model which offers passengers low-fare tickets by cutting down on services as for instance on-board meals, hub connectivity, and baggage transfer handling.[76] Following Southwest Airlines, a large number of low-cost carriers (LCCs) were founded around the globe such as AirTran, jetBlue, Ryanair, and easyJet.[77] Numerous market entries of LCCs intensified market competition and influenced price policies of many airlines. Air fares had to be decreased in order to stay competitive so that many airlines struggled to survive in the market.[78] Also, an unprecedented trend of market consolidation was experienced in the industry.[79]

In recent years, network carriers (NWCs), which traditionally provide passengers with comprehensive customer service, have more and more integrated the competitive low-cost business model in order to participate in this prospering market segment. NWCs have started to acquire existing LCCs (e.g. Lufthansa's acquisition of Germanwings in 2009), or established own low-cost subsidiaries (e.g. BMI's spin-off leading to the formation of bmibaby).[80] A similar strategic convergence can be observed in the low-cost segment where LCCs increasingly provide passengers with improved service quality. Because of various market entries in the low-cost segment, competition has picked up and the market has become fairly saturated. As a result, formerly pure differentiators started to offer complementary services on flights. Also new aircraft layouts including business class seating is nowadays apparent.[81] Correspondingly, the term "hybrid airlines", which describes airlines whose strategy combines aspects from traditional and low-cost business models, can often be found in recent scientific literature.[82]

In the course of increasing competition and intensifying price wars, the aviation industry has experienced a huge shift towards inter-organizational collaboration. This becomes evident in the fact that a large number of airlines have entered strategic alliances during the past decade. Today, members of the three airline alliances, namely Star Alliance, oneworld, and Sky Team, capture around 80% of the total market share.[83] The trend

[76] See Flenskow (2005), p. 102.
[77] In May 2011 AirTran was acquired by Southwest Airlines.
[78] See Goolsbee and Syverson (2008); Tan (2011).
[79] See Gillen (2006), p. 368; Bermig (2005), p. 20; Delfmann et al. (2005), pp. 4-5.
[80] bmibaby terminated its service in September 2012 after BMI's takeover by IAG.
[81] See Daraban (2012), p. 38; Klaas and Klein (2005), p. 138.
[82] See Ehmer et al. (2008), p. 13; Bieger and Agosti (2005), p. 41.
[83] See International Air Transport Association (2011), p. 1.

towards the creation of alliance constellations can be seen as a response to increasing market dynamics caused by previous deregulation of the global aviation sector. In order to counter rising market volatility, lower uncertainty, and reduce reaction time for competitive moves, leading airlines engaged in strategic alliances, and thereby decreased their own vulnerability to unexpected market developments.[84] Airline alliances often show a high degree of integration with alliance partners, including route coordination, revenue sharing, joint pricing, and marketing.[85]

3.1.2 Market players

The aviation industry encompasses several market participants. Analyzing the value chain reveals major market players, such as aircraft manufacturers, airlines, ground handlers, airport operators, and air traffic control (ATC), that contribute to the air transportation service. Given the complexity of the aviation industry this thesis limits its scope to the airline market. In the following, traditional types of airlines including their traditional business models are described.

NWCs are characterized by a large route network which is operated by a hub-and-spoke system to serve a wide range of destinations. As to date, NWCs constitute the leading type of airline capturing the largest market share in the aviation industry.[86] Within a hub-and-spoke network, airports at central locations (hubs) are strategically vital in order to collect traffic through so called feeder flights from various origins (spokes). In this way, passengers are accumulated at central locations so that larger airplanes can be used for long-haul flights to transfer passengers to the respective destinations.[87] In order to operate hub-and-spoke networks, NWCs are required to keep diverse fleet compositions consisting of various types of aircraft to operate short- and long-haul flights. Typically, airlines benefit from this network configuration through scale effects such as network extensions, increased utilization of airplanes, and a more efficient use of ground staff and equipment.[88] Moreover, NWCs are distinguished by the comprehensive customer service. In this regard, NWCs generally offer different passenger classes, including

[84] See Agusdinata and de Klein (2002), pp. 202-204.
[85] See Bermig (2005), p. 28.
[86] See Boeing (2012).
[87] See Gillen (2006), p. 369.
[88] See Auerbach and Delfmann (2005), pp. 76-79; Jäggi (2000).

economy, business, and first class. These passenger classes provide different service levels as for instance on-board service, in-flight entertainment, ticketing service, and passenger lounges at airports. Consequently, air fares are regularly in the upper price range claiming a premium price whereas most profits are generated from business- and long-haul travel.[89]

In contrast, LCCs usually operate a point-to-point network between smaller airports. These airports are often less congested which enables LCCs to reduce ground times and minimize holding patterns resulting in an improved on-time performance.[90] In order to provide low fares, LCCs inevitably need costs at a low level. Hence, LCCs normally charge passengers for in-flight service. Further cost savings result from the homogenous fleet composition. As LCCs predominantly operate short- and medium-haul flights in a point-to-point network, they are able to support their operations with only a limited number of different types of aircraft. In doing this, LCCs can reduce costs for maintenance, staff, and other overheads. In addition, a generally high seat density of airplanes enables LCCs to achieve high utilization rates and generate economies of scale.[91]

Similar to the low-cost business model, charter airlines follow a low-cost strategy by operating homogenous fleets with high density seating in a point-to-point network. In contrast, to LCCs, charter airlines usually provide some complementary on-board services such as meals, newspapers, and in-flight entertainment. Originally, charter airlines sold flights via tour operators as part of holiday packages and were therefore mainly focused on the tourism industry. For this reason, flight schedules usually change over the year due to seasonal demand, and temporary surcharges at peak travel times are common. Moreover, leisure travelers have been found to be more tolerant for longer distances to the departure airport which allows charter airlines to save costs by operating flights from selected airports.[92] Today, many charter airlines have been acquired by large tour operators and are fully integrated in their value chains.[93]

---

[89] See Gillen (2006), p. 369.
[90] See Bieger and Agosti (2005), p. 53.
[91] See Ehmer et al. (2008), p. 8.
[92] See Ehmer et al. (2008), p. 11.
[93] See Bieger and Agosti (2005), p. 54.

Regional airlines often follow a niche strategy by operating point-to-point flights between smaller airports on less competitive routes.[94] They also often generate revenues by conducting feeder flights to hub airports and thus support NWCs to operate hub-and-spoke networks. Travel distances are usually limited to short-haul flights so that the exclusive use of small aircraft mostly suffices.[95]

Besides passenger airlines, cargo airlines represent another large group of carriers within the aviation industry. Although cargo airlines do not directly compete with the preceding market players, there is a number of links between the market segments. In particular, belly cargo carried by passenger airlines constitutes a major field of competition. While cargo airlines are solely focused on the transportation of air freight, passenger airlines provide excess belly capacity of their aircraft as cargo space. Beyond that, large NWCs often operate own cargo divisions under their corporate umbrella and therefore compete directly with cargo airlines.[96] Unlike passenger airlines which usually operate round trips between two destinations, cargo airlines generally operate unidirectional flights to account for international trade flows. Therefore, deregulated air spaces providing high levels of freedom in air traffic are vital for their business operations.[97]

3.1.3 Price and demand mechanisms

The interdependency between price and demand is expressed by the price elasticity of demand. This concept describes the change in demand as a result from a given price change.[98] In order to assess the elasticity of demand, the change of demand after a 1% price increase has to be analyzed. If demand decreases disproportional after the price increase, demand is said to be elastic while an under-proportional decline in demand indicates an inelastic demand.[99] According to a study conducted by the EC in 2006, the demand in the aviation industry was found to have a low elasticity. More specifically, the EC expected only a marginal decrease of demand after an air fare increase due to a

---

[94] See Bieger and Agosti (2005), p. 53.
[95] See Ehmer et al. (2008), p. 11.
[96] Lufthansa Cargo, British Airways World and Air France / KLM Cargo are prominent examples of cargo airlines owned by NWC.
[97] See Ehmer et al. (2008), p. 12; For the Freedoms of Air refer to International Civil Aviation Organization (2004).
[98] See Gillen et al. (2003), p. 1.
[99] See InterVISTAS (2007), p. 2.

limited number of alternative modes of transportation.[100] However, a review of scientific literature about demand elasticity in aviation reveals that this presumption may be too general considering different types of passengers and flights in aviation. Against this background, it is suggested to analyze market segments individually and to distinguish between business and leisure travel as well as short, medium- and long-haul flights. This facilitates more qualified predictions about demand elasticity in the aviation industry. It is obvious that a more detailed elasticity assessment is required in order to make assumptions about demand reductions caused by substitution since the potential threat of alternative modes of transport differs significantly according to the travel distance. Gillen et al. conducted one of the most comprehensive studies on air travel demand elasticity. In their meta-study, Gillen et al. analyzed demand elasticity along distinct markets such as passenger type, trip purpose, and flight distance. In line with the previous remarks, Gillen et al. concluded that demand elasticity decreases with longer travel distances because of the decreasing number of effective substitutes. The study further states a lower price sensitivity of demand for business travelers compared to passengers on leisure trips. This was explained by more flexible trip planning and more thorough prize comparisons made by leisure travelers.[101] Beyond that, Brons et al. emphasized the value of time as an explanatory factor for differences of demand elasticity between both passenger types. They state that business travelers value the factor time more than leisure travelers. Time savings gained through air travel are more important and ticket prices have less influence on the purchase decision by business travelers so that fare increases have a smaller effect on their demand.[102] Competition intensity represents another influential factor for the demand elasticity in the aviation industry. In this regard, it is widely agreed that increasing competition leads to a higher price sensitivity of customers.[103] In aviation, particularly the market entry of LCCs which caused a significant decrease of average air fares on many routes has led to a growing number of price sensitive passengers in the industry.[104]

[100] See European Commission (2006), p. 37.
[101] See Gillen et al. (2003), pp. 1-2.
[102] See Brons et al. (2002), p. 168.
[103] See Gillen et al. (2003), p. 10.
[104] See Ernst & Young (2007), p. 78.

3.1.4 Industry trends

The aviation industry has experienced constantly changing market conditions over a long period of time. Similarly, a further dynamic industry evolution is projected for future years. For this reason, scholars are particularly affine to perform industry forecasts that try to anticipate industry trends and lower future uncertainty. The extant literature provides a number of major industry trends which are expected to change the current market environment. In the following, industry trends that can particularly influence airlines by coping with the EU-ETS are addressed.

As a driver of globalization which fosters commerce and communication while nurturing the global economic growth, air transportation is expected to be a key driver for further progress towards a globalized world. To improve international air operations, the aviation industry has already spawned some significant bilateral agreements across the world such as the EU-US Open Skies agreement, the Multilateral Agreement on Liberalization of International Air Transportation, and the ASEAN Multilateral Agreement on Air Services.[105] These treaties have turned a former highly regulated market into a globally accessible industry. Furthermore, several nations expressed the importance of a more deregulated market to support global economic growth. As a consequence of a more open international aviation market, market entry barriers will be further lowered and competition will continue to increase. Airlines will be less protected from international competitors through the retreat of national regulations. Also, the trend towards privatization of airlines is supposed to continue. More and more airlines will transform from nationally-owned organizations to international corporations.[106]

Moreover, air traffic growth is expected to continue which is expected to lead to severe capacity issues in the industry. Industry forecasts indicate an annual growth rate of 5% for passenger traffic and 5.2% for cargo traffic during the next two decades. In particular, forecasted growth for emerging economies, such as China, India, South-East Asia, and the Middle-East, is expected to be major contributors of this development.[107] However, there is a disturbing unbalance between the increasing demand for air transportation and the current market capacity of the aviation industry. More specifically, capacity

[105] See ASEAN (2009); European Union (2007); MALIAT (2001).
[106] See Doganis (2006), pp. 19-20.
[107] See Boeing (2012), p. 4.

bottlenecks at airports and within the air space are assumed to lead to congestion. Especially, hub airports at strategically important locations are expected to face issues with stands, runway slots, and the terminal infrastructure. Increased capacity issues are likely to become a major future challenge for airport operators and airlines operating at central airports.[108] The EC has tried to address the growing capacity problem by adopting the "Airport Package" which sets out a range of measures to improve slot allocation systems at airports.[109] There are also attempts to ease air space congestion under the Single European Sky ATM Research (SESAR). The SESAR program pursues to establish a new generation of Air Traffic Management System in Europe and promotes for instance Airport Collaborative Decision Making (A-CDM), an improved airport management concept to improve the information exchange between stakeholders at airports.[110]

The increasing emergence of LCCs has made air travel a viable alternative to other modes of transportation. LCCs have significantly lowered air fares on many routes so that air transportation has engaged in a serious competition with road and rail transportation. Success stories of Southwest Airways and Ryanair give rise to a promising future of this market segment. According to Airbus's Global Market Forecast, the low-cost segment will gain 5% market share over the next two decades leading to about 20% of the total market volume by 2031.[111] In addition, LCCs are expected to further expand their presence in the medium- and long-haul flight segment, which will further aggravate the downward trend of air fares and lower profit margins. Hence, cost-cutting measures are expected to become a vital instrument to stay competitive in the market.[112]

Furthermore, the public awareness about the consequences of climate change is expected to increase. Also, public support to lower GHG emissions in order to prevent global warming is projected to intensify. Therefore, the creation of a "green image" may become a competitive advantage for airlines as it helps to maintain legitimacy in the market. Airlines have already taken actions by promoting CO_2 offsetting programs in order to publicly acknowledge their responsibility for global warming.[113] Likewise, emission mitigation measures can be assumed at the political level. The enactment of

[108] See Doganis (2006), p. 25.
[109] See European Commission (2011b); de Witt and Burghouwt (2008).
[110] See EUROCONTROL (2013a).
[111] See Airbus (2012), p. 59.
[112] See Doganis (2006), pp. 24-25; Windle and Dresner (1999).
[113] See Albers et al. (2009), p. 5.

the Aviation Directive and inclusion of non-European airlines has put more pressure on the International Civil Aviation Organization (ICAO) to resume discussions about a global solution for aviation emissions. As a result, the ICAO recently demonstrated promising progress on the implementation of an international market-based mechanism to curb aviation emissions.[114]

3.2 Environmental policies in civil aviation

3.2.1 Convention on International Civil Aviation

The Convention on International Civil Aviation, also known as the Chicago Convention, is an early multilateral agreement in international aviation which was signed in December 1944. Its main objective was to define rules for airspace use and safety, and thereby achieve an enhanced coordination of international air travel. Yet, the convention parties were not able to agree on all predefined goals because of disagreements on the legal scope and the extent of liberalization induced by the convention. As a compromise, it was decided to formulate the "freedoms of the air" which specify different rights for flight operations in international aviation.[115] At the same time, the ICAO was established in order to promote and secure the future development of international aviation as a specialized agency of the UN. As of now, the ICAO has 191 members, however; unlike its individual member states, the EU has not signed the Chicago Convention and is thus not bound to its legislation.[116] The ICAO Council is the governing body which is entitled to set legally binding standards and recommend practices and procedures in international civil aviation for the convention parties.[117] As its main goal, the ICAO pursues to achieve a safe, secure, and sustainable development of civil aviation. Furthermore, environmental protection has become part of its responsibility whereas mitigating the impact of aviation-induced GHG emissions on the climate system constitutes one of the major environmental goals.[118] Nonetheless, as yet the ICAO has not lived up to its promises but has only managed to educate its members about the environmental impact

---

[114] See European Commission (2013f).
[115] See International Civil Aviation Organization (1944).
[116] See International Civil Aviation Organization (2013b).
[117] See International Civil Aviation Organization (1944), art. 37.
[118] See International Civil Aviation Organization (2012a); International Civil Aviation Organization (2012b); United Nations (1997), art. 2 (2).

of aviation on climate change. Legally binding measures that address GHG emission reductions in the global aviation industry have not been taken yet.

3.2.2 Aviation Directive

3.2.2.1 Motivation and objectives

In order to provide passengers with air transportation services, airlines are required to make huge capital investments for the acquisition of airplanes. Once the aircraft is in use, a significant amount of operating costs, especially fuel expenses, have to be covered. For this reason, there has been a constant necessity for technological and operational improvements in order to lower operating costs. In line with this, studies show that fuel efficiency levels have continuously increased in the aviation industry.[119] However, despite increased fuel efficiency, CO_2 emission trends show a reverse development due to the huge air traffic growth over the past years which could not be offset by the efficiency gains in the industry. The 4 figure shows the development of CO_2 emissions from aviation over the past decades:

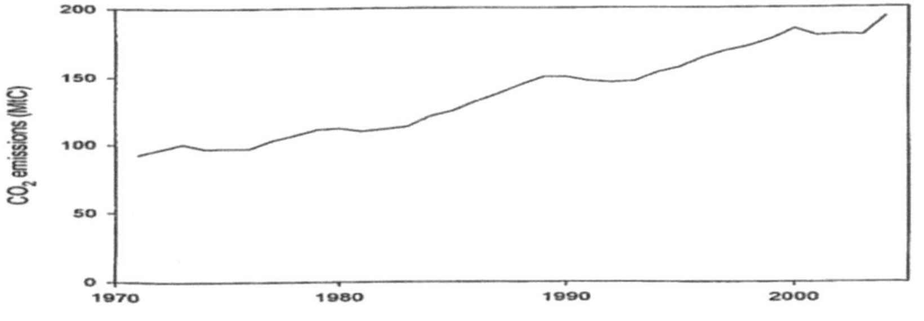

Figure 4: Global CO2 emissions from aviation (1970 - 2000) expressed in metric tons of carbon[120]

The EU had tried to raise global awareness about climate change and the contribution of GHGs for a long time. In this context, it was also pursued to urge the ICAO to reach a global solution for the increasing emissions from aviation. In its Sixth Community Environment Action Program the EU stated specific actions to meet its Kyoto emission

[119] See International Air Transport Association (2009).
[120] See World Bank (2006).

reduction targets which would include international aviation if the ICAO could not agree on a global resolution.[121] However, notable progress on a global agreement on the regulation of aviation emissions could not be achieved among the ICAO member states. As a consequence, the EU decided to amend the EU-ETS with the enactment of the Aviation Directive. Since 2012, all flights arriving at and departing from EEA airports have been included in the EU-ETS.[122] By taking this step, the EU expects to change travel behavior and to trigger operational and technological improvements that lower the environmental impact of air transportation.[123]

3.2.2.2 Major design elements

The Aviation Directive constitutes a scope extension of the original EU-ETS which includes aviation as the first segment of the transportation industry. In order to understand the implementation procedure and rules prescribed by the Directive, major design parameters are outlined in the following.

For the first trading period beginning in 2012, the Directive imposed an EEA-wide cap of 97% of the mean average annual CO_2 emissions of the years 2004 to 2006. This cap was reduced to 95% for the second period spanning from 2013 to 2020.[124]

Similar to the other EU-ETS sectors, the EU foresees a mix of free allowance allocation and auctioning to assign EUAs to airlines. The free allocation of EUAs is carried out by each member state applying a system-wide harmonized benchmark value. In the first period, 85% of the EUAs are allocated for free while the remaining 15% are assigned under auctioning. For the second trading period, a special reserve for fast-growing airlines and new entrants of 3% is retained, reducing the freely allocated EUAs to 82% and maintaining 15% for auctioning.[125]

In order to determine the quantity of free EUAs, airlines are required to submit verified Revenue Ton Kilometer (RTK) data from the monitoring year.[126] The monitoring year is

---

121 See European Council (2002b), art. 5 (2, iii).
122 See European Commission (2008), annex I (6).
123 See Anger and Köhler (2010), pp. 38-39.
124 See European Commission (2008), art. 3c (1-2).
125 See European Commission (2008), art. 3d, f.
126 A RTKs is defined as payload (t) x great circle distance (km) + 95 km. Whereas payload describes the actual revenue-generating portion of an aircraft's take-off weight and the great circle distance presents the shortest distance between the origin and the destination airport.

defined as the year ending 24 months before the trading period. In order to assign the respective quantity of EUAs to the airlines, RTKs from the monitoring year are multiplied by the benchmark value. This value is calculated by dividing the EEA-wide emission cap by the sum of the RTK flown in the monitoring year and thus expresses the number of EUAs per RTK.[127]

As an open cap-and-trade scheme, airlines are able to buy, sell or bank EUAs from every sector during the trading periods. Moreover, airlines are entitled to use international CERs and ERUs from clean-energy projects to cover CO_2 emissions up to a harmonized limit.[128] However, since CO_2 emissions from international aviation are not covered by the KP, airlines are not permitted to sell EUAs, which they received during the initial allocation, to parties outside the aviation sector to ensure correct accounting under the KP.[129]

After each trading period, airlines must surrender EUAs equivalent to their CO_2 emissions of the preceding year.[130] If the number of EUAs is not sufficient to cover the CO_2 emissions, penalties at a rate of € 100 per exceeding ton of CO_2 are imposed. In the following year, the airline is obliged to make up for the shortfall by reducing its CO_2 emissions accordingly.[131]

3.2.3 Current issues in climate policy for international aviation

According to the Aviation Directive, all flights operating to and from EEA airports are subject to the EU-ETS. This comprehensive approach which differentiates between European and non-European airlines was taken to avoid competitive distortions in the aviation industry.[132] However, a large consortium of airline associations and national governments, including the USA, China, India, and Russia heavily condemned the Aviation Directive. In particular, the imposition of the EU legislation on international aviation and its compliance to international law, such as the Chicago Convention, and

---

[127] See European Commission (2008), art. 3e.
[128] See European Commission (2008), art. 11a (1a); In 2012, airlines are allowed to use CERs and ERUs up to a limit of 15% of the allowances that have to be surrendered. Their use is restricted to 1.5% for the subsequent trading period.
[129] See European Commission (2008), preamble, supra note 27.
[130] See European Commission (2008), art. 12 (2a).
[131] See European Commission (2008), art. 16 (3).
[132] See European Commission (2008), annex I (6).

the principle of sovereignty of States were major controversial issues.[133] There has been a long-lasting debate concerning the legitimacy of the Aviation Directive. However, the EU as a community of states did not sign the Chicago Convention and is not member of the ICAO. Thus, the EU is entitled to make decisions about own initiatives on climate policy for aviation. In line with this, Advocate General Kokott approved the compliance of the Aviation Directive with international law.[134] In a final judgment the Court of Justice of the European Union declared the legitimacy of the Aviation Directive.[135] Despite this ruling, a coalition of almost 30 countries still opposed the imposition of the EU-ETS on non-EU airlines and developed a strategy that set out a range of counter measures. In a joint declaration, leading nations, including USA, China, and India, prohibited their national airlines to comply with the EU-ETS.[136] In addition, China took retaliation actions by freezing a USD$14 billion deal with the European aircraft manufacturer Airbus.[137] As a goodwill gesture, it was recently decided to suspend the inclusion of intercontinental flights until the next ICAO General Assembly in November 2013. This step was taken because of the progress made on a global market-based approach for aviation emissions at the last ICAO Council's meeting in November 2012. However, the EU reserves the right to reinforce the EU-ETS legislation. Depending on the eventual outcome for a global resolution later this year, the EU will decide to either exclude aviation from the EU-ETS to support an international market-based mechanism under the ICAO regime or to reapply the original Aviation Directive. Until then, all intra-EEA flights continue to be subject to the EU-ETS and EU law will be applied accordingly.[138]

---

[133] See High Court of Justice of England and Wales (2010).
[134] See Kokott (2011).
[135] See Court of Justice of the European Union (2011).
[136] See Joint Declaration of the Moscow meeting on inclusion of international civil aviation in the EU-ETS (2012).
[137] See Thomson Reuters (2012).
[138] See European Commission (2013f).

4 Impact analysis of the EU-ETS on the aviation industry

4.1 Focus of analysis and research approach

In order to depict the scope of impact of the EU-ETS on aviation and to increase analytical transparency, the following analysis takes three different perspectives on the industry to assess the impact on aviation. Chapter 4.2 comprises the individual perspective, which focuses on the impact on profitability for an individual airline. In this regard, different types of costs evoked by the EU-ETS are highlighted, possible pricing strategies after a cost increase are explained, and the potential to generate profit through the inclusion in the EU-ETS is examined. In chapter 4.3, the intra-industry perspective analyzes the impact on competition between airlines. In this context, possible competitive distortions between market players are unveiled. In particular, discriminating effects emerging from the applied allocation rule, varying business models, and divergent route networks coverage are analyzed. The collective industry perspective is taken in chapter 4.4, in which the analysis focus is on aspects concerning the overall industry. More specifically, the impact of the EU-ETS on technological, operational, and volume measures affecting the industry performance and the future development of the aviation industry are analyzed. Moreover, the potential industry-wide decline of demand through modal shifts by customers was evaluated. Figure 5 provides a structural overview of the described impact analysis:

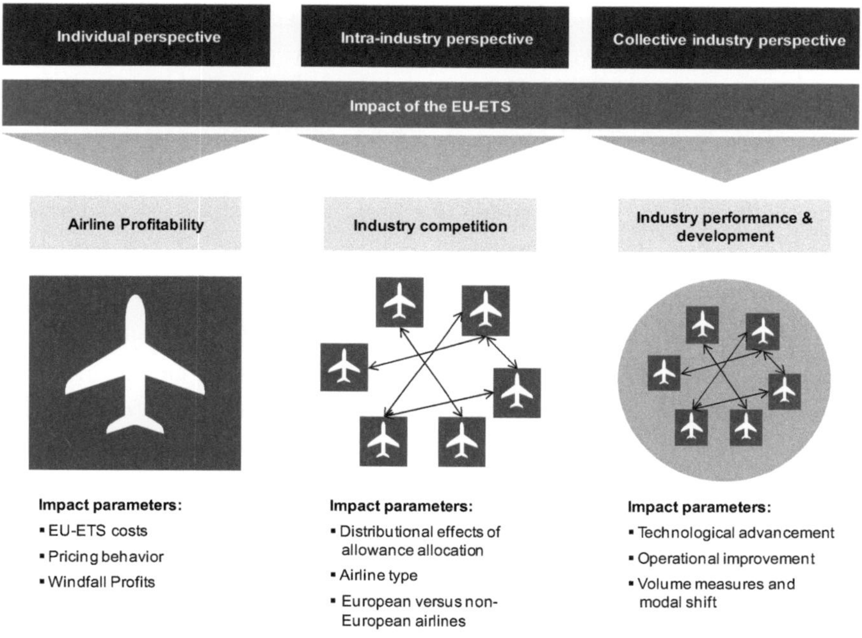

Figure 5: Analysis perspectives[139]

The existing literature in aviation research encompasses several scientific studies assessing the impact of the EU-ETS on aviation. These studies reveal that the EU-ETS impacts on the industry in many ways. However, most of the impact assessments take only a limited view by focusing on selected aspects of aviation. This makes it hard to understand the overall scope of impact on the aviation market. Building on this background, the following analysis incorporates results from a wide range of earlier impact assessments and related scientific publications to describe the scope of impact of the EU-ETS and highlight potential effects for the aviation industry.

In order to perform the impact analysis, a significant volume of literature was reviewed to find relevant contributions to the impact analysis of the EU-ETS for aviation. The review was primarily based on search results of the scientific database EBSCO's Business Source Complete and the scholarly search engine Google Scholar, which contain a

[139] Own illustration.

broad collection of peer-reviewed research journals and academic books. The literature search via databases was performed by using the keywords ("aviation", "emission", and "EU-ETS"). The keywords were either used in different combinations such as "aviation emission trading" and "aviation emission allowances" or were constructed into search strings such as "EU-ETS" AND "aviation". Due to the early stage of research on this topic, the literature review was not limited to a particular timeframe to incorporate the most possible number of relevant contributions. Furthermore, the analysis contains a number of publications from research institutions, governmental authorities and consultancy firms which were obtained through intense internet research.

In a first stage, titles and abstracts were screened in order to check for their relevance for the research focus of aviation and its inclusion in the EU-ETS, and to narrow down the number of publications contributing to the impact analysis. For cases in which a pre-screening of the article was not sufficiently conclusive for assessing its relevance for the analysis, a more detailed examination of the article was performed. In addition, reference sections of the relevant articles were screened in order to detect further literature sources that might have been neglected during the keyword search to achieve a higher level of completion. Finally, 33 articles remained from which 20 were identified as main articles providing input for the core statements and 13 articles were found to be supplementary, supporting the analysis in selected fields. A detailed description of the main articles as well as an overview of the supplementary literature is provided in the appendix.

In a next step, an in-depth literature evaluation was performed analyzing the remaining articles regarding research objective, research approach, underlying assumptions, and key findings. This allowed for a comparative analysis of the selected articles, which revealed similarities and helped to identify focal themes in current research. Subsequently, each research theme was analyzed to determine its specific impact on airlines. This helped to formulate three major impact fields describing the scope of impact on the aviation industry. At a more detailed level, sub-categories were formulated for each impact field, which increased the overall transparency of the analysis. Finally, assumptions about effects for the aviation industry were made based on the analysis results. The sequential analysis process is illustrated in the figure 6:

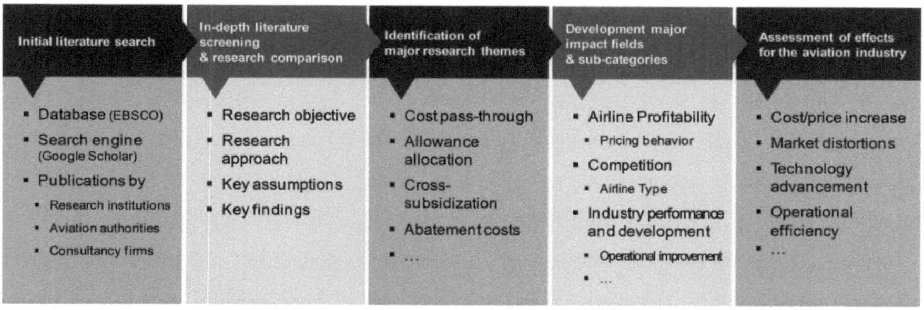

Figure 6: Research approach[140]

4.2 Airline profitability

4.2.1 EU-ETS costs

Since the enactment of the Aviation Directive, emission allowances have become a factor of production for airlines just like fuel, labor, and capital investments. Airlines are now exposed to additional costs which are supposed to affect the industry-wide profitability. For this reason, there is a range of studies in which EU-ETS-induced costs for aviation have been analyzed. The following describes cost factors which were identified to have an impact on airline profitability.

Besides the free allocation of emission allowances, the Aviation Directive foresees to auction a considerable proportion of EUAs to airlines. Auctioning is often seen as an effective approach to distribute emission allowances. Compared to benchmark allocation, auctioning does not require large amounts of emission data and therefore lowers administration costs. It presents a relatively inexpensive allocation method for policy makers and ensures a non-discriminatory allocation procedure for all participants and rewards low-emitting airlines. Most importantly, auctioning generates revenues which can be used for further emission reduction measures.[141] However, allowance allocation through auctioning requires airlines to engage in bidding contests so that acquisition costs for EUAs inevitably occur. To formulate an appropriate bid for the auction and minimize costs, airlines need to assess the carbon price and their potential costs that

[140] Own illustration.
[141] See Wit et al. (2005), p. 9.

would emerge from emission reductions. In support of this position, Boon et al. state that airlines take all actions to curb emissions as long as they are less expensive than the acquisition of EUAs on the carbon market and the required costs of auctioning.[142] Yet, high abatement costs may prevent airlines from taking effective emission mitigation actions, thus airlines are instead expected to become net buyers of EUAs.[143] This implies that airlines acquire EUAs through auctioning and secondary trading to cover CO_2 emissions rather than lowering emission levels. In particular, the projected growth of air traffic is expected to increase CO_2 emissions which may result in scarcity of EUAs for airlines. Therefore, auctioning is likely to become an important source of emission allowances in order to cover CO_2 emissions that exceed the freely allocated EUAs.[144] Most EUAs are auctioned on the European Energy Exchange (EXX).[145] To receive EUAs on the EXX, airlines need to participate in a competitive tender procedure in which a so called sealed-bid auction is applied. The latter means that airlines submit bids for a specific number of EUAs without knowing the bids of their competitors. In order to allocate the EUAs after the tender procedure, the Auction Clearing Price is determined which represents the lowest bid that still receives EUAs. Since the EU Auction Regulation prescribes a uniform-price format, EUAs are sold at the Auction Clearing Price regardless of the specific bids submitted by the participants.[146] This price is supposed to be close to the spot price on the carbon market assuming a perfect market and thus arbitrage profits caused by price differentials for EUAs are unlikely.[147] As it can be seen, the overall cost burden of auctioning will be significantly influenced by the future development of the carbon price. As a consequence of the common EU-ETS carbon market, auctioning costs are directly affected by economic conditions in other EU-ETS sectors. More specifically, growing demand for EUAs in other EU-ETS sectors as a result of increased economic activity causes an increase of the carbon price and consequently an increased Auction Clearing Price. Nonetheless, due to the temporary exclusion of in- and outbound EEA flights from the EU-ETS, which makes up a significant share of EUAs foreseen to be auctioned to airlines, the EU requested to defer the auctioning of

[142] See Boon et al. (2007), p. 2.
[143] See Mendes and Santos (2008), p. 206.
[144] See Ernst & Young (2007), p. 20; Wit et al. (2005), p. 122.
[145] See European Commission (2011c); Germany, Poland and the United Kingdom opted out and operate own auction platforms.
[146] See European Commission (2010), art. 5; Hepburn et al. (2006), pp. 144-145.
[147] See Boon et al. (2007), p. 43; Wit et al. (2005), p. 135.

EUAs by the EEX until clarity about the number of airlines that make use of the derogation pursuant for international flights is achieved.[148]

As a constantly growing industry, aviation is assumed to be heavily involved in market transactions on the spot market. Consequently, the carbon price as a cost indicator will become increasingly important. As stated earlier, the carbon price has been fairly volatile since the beginning of the EU-ETS. Hence, hedging techniques, such as trading with future contracts, are nowadays a common risk management practice to limit risk exposure. Also, auctioning is expected to set a price signal and act as a price floor, and thereby contribute to more price stability on the spot market.[149] However, slowing economic activity in previous years has led to a huge built-up of emission allowances across many EU-ETS sectors so that a repeated slump of the carbon price is expected.[150] This price fall is anticipated despite the inclusion of aviation and the projected increase of demand for EUAs because aviation is supposed to have only a minor impact on the carbon price in the open trading system.[151] In its recent proposal the EC states to take intervening actions to prevent a further decline of the carbon price which may otherwise undermine the effectiveness of the EU-ETS.[152] These measures are assumed to counter a further downward trend of the allowance price. In conclusion, it can be said that the carbon price is likely to constitute an increasingly important cost factor for the aviation industry. In particular, future predictions, such as the ongoing growth of air traffic and the further decrease of the EU-ETS emission cap, will raise the significance of carbon trading as an operative measure in the aviation industry.

The existing literature only reveals little information about administration and transaction costs associated with the EU-ETS. These costs are often excluded from current impact assessments as they are not supposed to have a meaningful impact on airline profits.[153] Yet, to provide a most complete impact analysis they should be addressed at this point. The EU-ETS induces administration and transaction costs on airlines in different ways. For the allowance allocation under benchmarking, airlines are required to assign additional resources to receive free EUAs, such as personnel, to ensure a constant monitor-

[148] See European Commission (2013g).
[149] See Hepburn et al. (2006), p. 138.
[150] See European Commission (2012b), p. 5.
[151] See Anger and Köhler (2010), p. 44.
[152] See European Commission (2012b).
[153] See Wit et al. (2005), p. 130.

ing and reporting of emission data for submission to the regulatory authorities.[154] Similarly, auctioning requires resources to formulate and submit bids to participate in tender procedures.[155] Furthermore, airlines need to cover transaction costs that occur through trading activities on the carbon market. As the clearing house, the EXX charges several service fees for the provision and the conduct of allowance trading such as opening fees for registry accounts, exchange fees for EUA trading, and clearing fees for the transaction.[156] Brokerage fees are due in cases where carbon market transactions are carried out by an intermediary trading company.[157]

Unlike the aforementioned costs that are directly induced through the EU-ETS, abatement costs represent a cost type that emerges from emission mitigation actions taken as response to the EU legislation. In this context, scholars name technical, operational, and volume measures that airlines might take to reduce emissions.[158] However, the incentive to reduce emissions is highly dependent on the carbon price. This implies that airlines base the decision on whether to invest in new technology or to improve operational efficiency to decrease carbon emissions on the costs of EUAs.[159] In other words, airlines will abate emissions as long as abatement costs are still lower than or equal to the costs incurring from buying EUAs on the carbon market.[160] From this it can be concluded that the price for one EUA constitutes the threshold for the maximum amount to be spent on mitigation measures reducing CO_2 emissions by one metric ton. In this context, it is often referred to the marginal abatement cost curve which helps to determine the additional costs emerging from an emission reduction by one unit. It therefore indicates the quantity of EUAs that can be saved for a particular mitigation measure which provides support for the investment decision.[161] In general, abatement costs in aviation are high compared to other EU-ETS sectors. Airlines are usually required to make huge investments

[154] See Ibid.
[155] See Hepburn et al. (2006), p. 146.
[156] See European Energy Exchange (2013b).
[157] See Wit et al. (2005), p. 130.
[158] See Boon et al. (2007), p. 13.
[159] See Boon et al. (2007), p. 2.
[160] See Oxera (2003), p. 18.
[161] See Morris et al. (2009), p. 6.

in order to reduce CO_2 emissions.[162] Assuming the current price for the future does not suggest significant mitigation actions from airlines in the future.[163]

4.2.2 Pricing behavior

The imposition of emission allowances on aviation is assumed to affect the costs of air transportation across the entire aviation industry. EU-ETS-evoked costs are expected to result in increasing airfares which will adversely affect the profitability of airlines.[164] The following formula was conceptualized by Anger and Köhler illustrating the key drivers for fare changes which helps to understand the impact of EUAs on airfares:[165]

$$\Delta\, \mathrm{pi,j} = \frac{\mathrm{FUi,j} \times \mathrm{c} \times \mathrm{pa}}{\mathrm{LF,j}} \times \mathrm{CF}$$

The formula shows that a change in airfares (Δ p) by using a particular aircraft type (i) over a certain distance (j) is defined by the amount of fuel used over the distance (FUi,j), the amount of carbon emissions released (c), the allowance price (pa), and the load factor (LF) of the aircraft. The cost pass-through rate (CF), which is the degree to which additional costs are passed on to the consumer, has a significant impact since it determines the actual fare change for the passenger. The degree to which costs are passed on to the passenger depends on financial factors, i.e. the airline's capacity to absorb costs while sustaining profitability and its pricing behavior, as explained in the following.

Competition intensity is in many ways related to the prevailing price policy in a market segment since it often determines the price premium that can be asked from the customer. It also determines the extent to which extra costs can be offset by revenues without jeopardizing profitability.[166] It is often claimed that the aviation industry is highly competitive and airlines are therefore forced to apply marginal cost-based pricing. Hence, those studies assume that airlines pass any cost increase fully to the passenger.[167] In line with this presumption, other studies stress the low profit margins in the

[162] See Winchester et al. (2011).
[163] For the latest price level please refer to EEX (2013a).
[164] See Vivid Economics (2008); Boon et al. (2007); Frontier Economics (2006).
[165] See Anger and Köhler (2010), p. 40.
[166] See Malina et al. (2012), p. 38.
[167] See Vivid Economics (2008); Frontier Economics (2006); European Commission (2006); Wit et al. (2005).

aviation industry to be a major factor which forces airlines to recover additional costs from the passenger.[168] However, these assumptions may be over-simplified and are derived from unrealistic conditions for the aviation industry, such as perfect competition and demand-driven supply.[169]

Ernst & Young opposed the assumption of perfect competition in the aviation industry. In their impact assessment they argued that the European airline industry has characteristics that rather suggest oligopolistic and monopolistic market structures.[170] In this regard, Forsyth delved deeper into competitive conditions by analyzing individual routes in the airline industry. In support of Ernst & Young, it was found that flight routes feature different market structures of competitive, oligopolistic, and monopolistic nature which have a varying effect on the cost pass-through rate and the corresponding increase of air fares.[171] Malina et al. described monopolistic markets as low density routes on which typically only a single airline operates. Due to the lack of competition, fares usually exceed costs so that airlines are more likely to absorb additional costs.[172] However, studies indicate that monopoly power in the airline industry is often weak because of the large number of alternative flight connections. Monopolistic market conditions on a direct flight can be easily substituted by combined flights, including a stopover. Hence, monopolistic market structures on particular routes do not necessarily guarantee highly profitable air operations.[173] In order to keep high profit margins, airlines could be willing to pass costs on to the passenger. However; on monopolistic routes fares are already high and often easily substitutable by transit options so that a fare increase would likely result in a severe decline of demand. A study by Vivid Economics states that airlines inevitably suffer a decrease in profits on monopolistic flight routes either through declining demand or lower profit margins.[174]

It was found that oligopolistic market structures present the more general case for flight routes in international aviation. This competitive situation exists if a limited number of

---

168 See Boon et al. (2007); PricewaterhouseCoopers (2005); Competition Commission (2002).
169 See Oxera (2003), p. 4.
170 See Ernst & Young (2007), p. 12.
171 See Forsyth (2008), p. 18.
172 See Malina et al. (2012), p. 38.
173 See Forsyth (2008), p. 18; InterVISTAS (2007), p. 5.
174 See Vivid Economics (2008), p. 11.

airlines compete on a particular route.[175] Forsyth analyzed Bertrand and Cournot strategies to explain typical pricing behavior of market participants in an oligopolistic market.[176] In a Bertrand competition which assumes that prices are set at the level where profits are maximized, airlines would initially fully absorb the extra costs despite facing temporary losses. Consequently, airlines that do not have the financial strengths to offset these costs would be forced to exit the market. In the long run, airlines would restore profitability through gradual fare increases under eased competitive conditions. The Cournot model assumes that prices are determined by the optimal quantity of products or services that need to be sold by a firm. Prices are usually set above marginal costs which enable market players to generate oligopoly rents. In this case, Forsyth expected EU-ETS costs to be shared by airlines and passengers which results in a more modest fare increase. Yet, Forsyth further noted that due to relatively high fare levels this pricing strategy could stimulate increasing competition in the long run through new market entries of airlines on these routes.[177]

The constant increase of air traffic has reached capacity limits at many airports.[178] As a result, the steadily increasing demand for air transportation can hardly be satisfied due to capacity constraints in flight movements that can be currently operated at central airports. When market supply is limited, firms usually try to maximize yields by setting the price at a level where demand equals the maximum supply (Demand Clearance Pricing).[179] In aviation this would mean that airlines increase airfares up to a level at which passenger numbers equal the maximum number of flights that can be operated from an airport with limited capacity.[180] As a consequence, costs are likely to be absorbed by the airline since air fares are already set at a maximum to utilize airplanes and therefore further price increases cannot be imposed without causing significant retreat of demand. Scholars expect decreasing profits especially on connections involving congested airports.[181]

---

[175] See Forsyth (2008), p. 18; Ernst & Young (2007), p. 12.
[176] A detailed definition of both price strategies provide Qin and Stuart (1997).
[177] See Forsyth (2008), p. 21.
[178] See Ernst & Young (2007), pp. 56-57; Mott McDonald (2006), chapter 7.
[179] See Oxera (2003), p. 4.
[180] Bieger and Agosti state that pricing strategies can differ for flights including transits at hub airports despite congestion because of fierce competition with point-to-point connections. See Bieger and Agosti (2005), p. 50.
[181] See Ernst & Young (2007), p. 14; Oxera (2003), pp. 5-7.

As mentioned above, the potential demand response after a fare increase has a major impact on the extent to which extra costs can be passed on to the passenger. Consequently, the price elasticity of demand deserves closer attention in order to assess the pricing behavior of airlines in response to the inclusion in the EU-ETS. Scientific literature provides opposing views on the demand elasticity for air travel. In its impact assessment, the EC suggested an only marginal decline of demand for European airlines after a potential fare increase assuming a low price elasticity of demand for air transport.[182] In contrast, Ernst & Young stressed a significant impact on profit margins for European carriers due to a considerable decline of demand after a price increase following the inclusion in the EU-ETS.[183] However, these assumptions about the demand elasticity are too general in order to draw conclusions about the impact on profitability of airlines. In fact, airlines are differently affected by the costs induced through the EU-ETS. The respective business model has a significant effect on the potential cost recovery from the passenger as explained in later remarks.

From the preceding remarks it can be concluded, that the imposition of the EU-ETS regulatory is likely to adversely affect the profitability of airlines. Depending on the competition intensity on individual routes, airlines apply different pricing strategies which determine the rate of EU-ETS costs that are passed through to air fares. In this regard, airlines might be differently impacted by the EU-ETS because of different levels of price sensitivity of passengers. Yet, losses may inevitably occur for all airlines resulting either from declining demand or additional costs that have to be offset by revenues. The increasing number of congested airports forces airlines to apply discriminating pricing strategies in order to maximize yields. This may limit the potential to enforce further price increases and consequently cause lower profit margins. Especially where demand is highly elastic, airlines might not be able to pass additional costs on to the passenger. Therefore, airlines need to conduct airfare changes under the consideration of potential demand response to optimize the cost recovery rate and to sustain demand.

[182] See European Commission (2006), p. 37.
[183] See Ernst & Young (2007).

4.2.3 Windfall profits

The inclusion of aviation in the EU-ETS is widely assumed to increase the cost burden on airlines. However, some studies suggest that the imposition of allowance rights can create a new source of profit for airlines.[184] Through the free allocation of EUAs, airlines may benefit from windfall profits which are generated through an increase of air fares at an unchanged cost base.[185] Yet, windfall profits are highly dependent on the applied allocation procedure as they can only be achieved under grandfathering and benchmarking which do not require investments for emission allowances by the airlines.[186]

The economic justification for generating windfall profits can be explained with the concept of opportunity costs. According to this theory, freely allocated emission allowances entail opportunity costs for the permit owner. These are the costs of using the allowances in order to cover CO_2 emissions instead of selling the emissions allowances on the carbon market. Although EUAs may be used to cover CO_2 emissions, the overall operational costs have increased. If opportunity costs are passed on to the customer, windfall profits are generated.[187] In this context, Wit et al. refered to "scarcity rents" that are created by setting a stringent emission cap which eventually leads to EUA scarcity. They further noted that the high share of freely allocated EUAs enables the permit owner to capture most of these rents.[188]

Because of the fierce price competition in aviation, opportunity costs are often assumed to be passed on to their full extent.[189] This would potentially result in high windfall profits for airlines given the major share of 82% that the EU foresees to allocate for free during the current trading period.[190] A contradictory view take Ernst & Young by claiming that the high price sensitivity of customers in aviation does not allow for further air fare increases. In their opinion, windfall profits are therefore not expected to arise in the aviation sector.[191] Other studies which analyzed different allocation methods argued that opportunity benefits may arise, which have an adverse impact on windfall profits. In

[184] See Vivid Economics (2008); Boon et al. (2007); European Commission (2006).
[185] See Sijm et al. (2006).
[186] See Wit et al. (2005), pp. 162-163.
[187] See Wråke et al. (2010), p. 332; Wit et al. (2005), pp. 162-163.
[188] See Wit et al. (2005), p. 163.
[189] See Boon et al. (2007), p. 31; Wit et al. (2005), p. 134.
[190] See European Commission (2008), art. 3d.
[191] See Ernst & Young (2007).

these situations, airlines have the opportunity to receive more EUAs in future periods by increased emissions in the current period. It is argued that those opportunity benefits largely offset the opportunity costs so that no price increase is imposed.[192] Yet, opportunity benefits require allocation methodologies that apply constantly updated emission data for the allocation of emission allowances. The current benchmark rule follows a rather static approach which allocates EUAs according to CO_2 emissions of a specific monitoring year without future updating. Hence, opportunity benefits are unlikely to be achievable in the near future.[193]

4.3 Industry competition

4.3.1 Distributional effects of allowance allocation

Although auctioning represents the default allocation method for emission allowances within the EU-ETS, the Aviation Directive prescribes only an auction share of 15%. Airlines will obtain the vast majority of EUAs free of costs until the end of the current trading period in 2020.[194] An analysis of free allocation methods for emission allowances unveils discriminating distributional effects. In the following, free allocation rules are described and examined regarding potential competitive distortions. This helps to underline the impact of the applied allocation rule on the competition in the aviation industry.

There are different types of free allocation rules that can be used for the distribution of emission allowances. Grandfathering describes the free allocation of allowances based on historical emissions usually with reference to a single year, an average value for a past time period or a maximum value of preceding years.[195] Since its adoption, EUAs for stationary installations had been predominantly allocated through grandfathering carried out in accordance to NAPs of each member state.[196] Hereby, EUAs were allocated based on average emission values of past time periods.[197] The aviation industry,

---

[192] See Boon et al. (2007), pp. 9-10; Neuhoff et al. (2006); Sijm et al. (2005), p. 45.
[193] See Malina et al. (2012), p. 37.
[194] See European Commission (2008), art. 3d.
[195] See Faber et al. (2007), p. 17.
[196] See Jegou and Rubini (2011), p. 6.
[197] See Neuhoff et al. (2006); As an example, Germany's baseline period for the first and second trading period was based on historical emissions from 2000-2002 and 2000-2005, respectively.

however, is susceptible to exogenous factors which make emission levels particularly volatile. Aside from macroeconomic events, factors like epidemics, terrorist attacks, and environmental disasters, affect air travel activity. Hence, the use of a relatively long baseline period, capturing emission data of several years, has to be ensured in order to obtain representative emission values for the allowance allocation.[198] However, the ex-post allocation of allowances based on average historical emission data can put strong growing airlines at a disadvantage over competitors. Despite decreasing dominance, incumbent carriers may receive a comparatively large proportion of free EUAs by benefiting from a high market share in the past. In contrast, LCCs that have shown high annual growth rates in most recent years are likely to face an under-allocation of free EUAs.[199] In addition, grandfathering strongly contradicts the "polluter-pays principle" as it favors large emitters and discriminates airlines that already decreased emission levels in the past.[200] LCCs usually operate a young fleet which is characterized by low emission levels. As a result, they would likely receive fewer EUAs.[201] In response to that, the European Low Fares Airline Association condemned the use of the grandfathering method for emission allowances in order to ensure equity for LCCs.[202]

The Aviation Directive prescribes to apply a benchmarking scheme for the free allocation of EUAs. Similar to grandfathering, benchmarking includes emission data from past time periods in order to allocate EUAs. However, it further uses benchmark factors which are industry-specific performance measures. Under this rule, low-emitting airlines that have taken early actions against carbon pollution can be rewarded. Also, benchmarking seeks to encourage large emitters to invest in new technologies and thus lower emissions.[203] It can be differentiated between input, output, and technology-based benchmarking methods. These benchmarking types take different performance indicators to allocate emission allowances such as efficiency measures, industry-specific output factors, and fleet characteristics.[204] A typical input-based benchmark indicator used in aviation is Available Ton Kilometer (ATK) which describes the total fleet capacity

---

[198] See Faber et al. (2007), p. 17.
[199] See Morrell (2007), p. 5566; New entrants would not receive any free EUAs under this approach.
[200] See Faber et al. (2007), p. 17; The polluter-pays-principle advocates that the polluter is responsible to pay for the environmental damage that he has caused.
[201] See Faber et al. (2007), p. 32; Frontier Economics (2006), p. 15.
[202] See European Low Fares Airline Association (2006); Frontier Economics (2006), pp. 57, 63.
[203] See Faber et al. (2007), p. 18.
[204] See Faber et al. (2007), p. 24.

of airlines.[205] RTKs are used as a benchmark indicator for output-based benchmarking. This is a measurement for freight and passenger weight transported over a certain distance.[206] Under the Aviation Directive, the EU prescribes a one-off output-based benchmarking approach based on the average historical emission levels of 2004 to 2006.[207] One-off benchmarking describes the free allocation of perpetual emission allowances ahead of the trading period.[208] In order to calculate the benchmark factor, the historical CO_2 emissions (2004 - 2006) are reduced by the auctioning share of 15% and the proposed emission reductions of each trading period (3% in 2012 and 5% in 2013 - 2020). The remaining number is then divided by the total RTK of the monitoring year 2010 as illustrated in the following formula:[209]

$$\text{Benchmark} = \frac{(1 - \text{quota of auctioned allowances}) \text{ X } (1 - \text{reduction quota}) \text{ X } \sum_{i=1}^{n} \text{average annual emissions}_{2004-2006}}{\sum_{i=1}^{n} \text{RTK of the monitoring year 2010}}$$

Subsequently, the actual annual quantity of EUAs for each airline can be determined by multiplying the benchmark factor with the individual RTKs in 2010.[210] However, similar to the aforementioned distorting effects under the grandfathering approach, the current benchmark methodology can potentially lead to inequity between airlines by fixing the EUA allocation to historical CO_2 emissions until the end of the third trading period.[211] Additionally, there will be no updating of the monitoring year until 2020.[212] Hence, the current one-off benchmarking method does not account for recent industry developments and may put strong growing airlines at a competitive disadvantage. The aviation industry has been steadily growing at an approximate annual rate of 5%.[213] This growth

205 See Faber et al. (2007), pp. 26-28; ATKs are calculated by capacity (t) x total distance flown (km).
206 See Faber et al. (2007), p. 10.
207 See Malina et al. (2012), p. 37.
208 See Boon et al. (2007), p. 8; Indeed, one off benchmarking that sets perpetual rights is an extreme form of allocation methodologies, hence in order to maintain fairness and provide a finite horizon for allocation amounts, Åhman et al. (2005) suggest a "ten-year rule". Under the Aviation Directive free EUAs have been determined until 2020.
209 See Scheelhaase et al. (2010), p. 18; For the period 2013-2020 an additional special reserve of 3% for fast-growing airlines and new entrants must be subtracted from the average historical emissions.
210 See European Commission (2008), art. 3e.
211 See European Commission (2008), art. 3c.
212 See European Commission (2008), art. 3d (3); An updated benchmarking would reflect dynamic market evolution. However, environmentally the approach is highly disputable since it fosters the perverse incentives to purposely curtail emission reductions in the current trading period to obtain more emission allowances in the future period. See Betz and Sato (2006), p. 352; Hepburn et al. (2006), pp. 142-143.
213 See Boeing (2012), p. 4.

has mainly been captured by the low-cost market segment whose market share has increased by about 25% since 2004.[214] Therefore, it can be assumed that EUA scarcity will be more severe for LCCs as they need to cover growth-induced carbon emission increases. In conclusion, one-off benchmarking is likely to adversely affect growing airlines due to its lacking consideration of dynamic market developments in the industry.[215]

An assessment of the applied output parameter unfolds further competitive disadvantages for LCCs. At first sight, one would probably assume higher efficiency values for LCCs because of the generally high seat density and young, fuel efficient fleet compositions. However, despite highly utilized airplanes on short-haul flights, studies show that LCCs could face more issues to cover CO_2 emissions due to the favorable conditions for long-haul flights under the allocation method.[216] NWCs usually carry huge amounts of belly cargo on long-haul flights so that load factors significantly increase. In addition, the small share of high-emission flight phases, such as take-off and landing, as well as the usage of larger airplanes, lead to high fuel efficiency on long-haul flights.[217] As NWCs operate a large number of long-haul flights within hub-and-spoke systems, they might be able to benefit from the applied benchmarking rule. Especially non-European NWCs whose short-haul feeder flights are not subject to the EU-ETS are likely to receive a proportionately higher share of free EUAs and gain a competitive advantage. In order to resolve discriminating effects of benchmark allocation, it has already been suggested to conduct separate benchmarks for short- and long-haul flights.[218] Moreover, the EU recently decided to temporarily exclude international flights into and out of the EEA from the EU-ETS. As a result, most long-haul flights are currently excluded from the scheme and it will depend on the progress made by the ICAO on a global solution against aviation emissions if the aforementioned effects will reoccur later this year.[219]

[214] See Airbus (2012), p. 81.
[215] See Frontier Economics (2006), p. 64.
[216] See Morrell (2007).
[217] See Mendes and Santos (2008), p. 201; Faber et al. (2007), p. 22.
[218] See Scheelhase et al. (2010).
[219] See European Commission (2013f).

4.3.2 Airline type

The previous section gave first insights about distorting effects of the EU-ETS on competition in the aviation industry. Most of the competitive distortions emerge from the distinct peculiarities of the varying business models regarding passenger type and route network. Previous research has predominantly focused on differences concerning the impact of the EU-ETS on NWCs and LCCs. Hence, the following analysis is limited to the results found in the literature review and thus excludes other airline types.

It is broadly known that NWCs and LCCs differ significantly regarding the passenger structure because NWCs have a much higher share of business travelers than LCCs.[220] There are notable differences in demand elasticity between passenger groups. A common finding in scientific literature is that business passengers are less sensitive to price than passengers on leisure trips.[221] In addition, NWCs are likely to take advantage of different passenger classes that they provide in order to satisfy heterogeneous customer needs. Unlike many LCCs, NWCs offer distinct fare classes, including economy, business, and first class. Studies show that demand elasticity is lower for passengers travelling business and first class than passengers in economy class. Scheelhaase and Grimme explained this deviation with higher ticket prices for these travel classes and usually higher income level in this passenger segment. Consequently, NWCs are able to strategically pass extra costs on to less price sensitive passengers and thus ease adverse demand effects.[222]

Aside from varying passenger structures, NWCs are likely to benefit from their route network configuration. As mentioned earlier, NWCs usually operate hub-and-spoke networks including short- and medium-haul feeder flights to accumulate passengers at hub airports and achieve higher utilization rates on long-haul flights.[223] This means that NWCs have a notable number of transit passengers on short- and medium-haul flights that in fact travel on intercontinental connections. In this regard, Scheelhaase et al. found that only about 40% of Lufthansa's long-haul passengers originate from its hubs in

[220] See Scheelhaase and Grimme (2007), p. 261.
[221] See Gillen (2003); Brons et al. (2002).
[222] See Scheelhaase and Grimme (2007), p. 260.
[223] See Gillen (2006), p. 368.

Frankfurt and Munich while the remaining 60% are transferred from feeder flights.[224] Studies suggest a relatively low demand elasticity for transit passengers on feeder flights as it usually represents only a small proportion of the total flight ticket.[225] For this reason, it is fair to assume that demand for short-haul flights is less elastic for NWCs than for LCCs that operate predominantly point-to-point connections. In addition to transit passengers, NWCs provide service for a considerable number of long-haul passengers on direct flights. Similar to transit passengers, Gillen found long-haul passengers to be less price sensitive than passengers on shorter distances due to the diminishing number of substitutes with increasing distance travelled.[226]

In general, it can be concluded that the overall price sensitivity of passengers travelling with NWCs is lower than for the low-cost customer segment. In line with this, Ernst & Young project a severe impact on the profitability of LCCs as a cause of declining demand after a fare increase induced by the EU-ETS.[227] Moreover, NWCs might be able to use their diverse passenger structure to mitigate the impact on demand after a fare increase. NWCs could pass extra costs on to less price sensitive passengers while lowering fare increases for others. On the contrary, LCCs have a comparatively homogenous passenger structure and therefore no possibility to redistribute costs on less price sensitive passengers. This might lead to a decreasing price differential between LCCs and NWCs for flights on competing routes. As a result, demand on flights operated by LCCs might reduce and some demand shifts to NWCs might be experienced.[228] Ernst & Young expect the low-cost segment to lose around half of its passengers by 2022 due to the linking of aviation to the EU-ETS.[229]

In addition, the temporary exclusion of flights into and out of the EEA leads to discriminating effects in the European aviation market. Under current legislation, only intra-EEA flights need to be covered by EUAs. A comparison of Ryanair and Lufthansa shows that Europe's largest LCC emits about 97.5% of its total CO_2 emission within the EU while Lufthansa's share only accounts for 28%.[230] It becomes obvious that under the current

[224] See Scheelhaase et al. (2010), p. 16.
[225] See Morrell (2007), p. 5570; Frontier Economics (2006), p. 72.
[226] See Gillen (2003).
[227] See Ernst & Young (2007), p. 37.
[228] See Forsyth (2008), p. 24.
[229] See Ernst & Young (2007), p. 35.
[230] See Scheelhaase and Grimme (2007), p. 260.

exclusion of intercontinental flights LCCs face a competitive disadvantage over NWCs because of their intra-European route network. LCCs have to cover a larger share of their flights with EUAs than NWCs. The ultimate decision concerning the ongoing debate about the implementation of a market-based mechanism against aviation emissions at the ICAO level will therefore have an influential effect on the competition between European airlines.

4.3.3 European versus non-European airlines

Although the Aviation Directive pursues a non-discriminatory principle and tries to prevent carbon leakage, regional schemes inevitably affect competitiveness and trigger unwanted strategic behavior.[231] In the following, distorting effects on competition between European- and non-European airlines arising from the geographical scope of the EU-ETS legislation are analyzed.

In its original form, the Aviation Directive includes flights leaving from and arriving in the EEA besides flights within the EEA.[232] As a result, also non-European carriers need to acquire EUAs for European routes. However, the vast majority of flights are usually operated outside the EEA. Therefore, non-European airlines may have a competitive advantage over European airlines under the EU-ETS. In line with this, a comparison of US-and European NWCs by Scheelhaase et al. revealed that US NWCs benefit from the location of their hub airports. European NWCs do not only have to surrender EUAs for long-haul flights departing from hub airports located in the EEA but also have to cover all CO_2 emissions from short-haul feeder flights. US NWCs, however, operate feeder flights outside the EEA and are therefore excluded from the EU legislation.[233] Consequently, European NWCs need to acquire a much bigger proportion of EUAs in order to cover emissions and therefore face a larger impact on operating costs by the EU-ETS. In this regard, Scheelhaase and Grimme found that Lufthansa has to cover more than 92% of its flights with EUAs.[234] Additionally, Scheelhaase et al. argued that the low load factor and the use of less fuel efficient aircraft on short-haul flights is likely to be disadvanta-

---

[231] See Faber and Brinke (2011), p. 10; Carbon leakage is defined as an increase of CO_2 in one country or region as a result of an emission reduction policy in another.
[232] See European Commission (2008), preamble, par. 16.
[233] See Scheelhaase et al. (2010), pp. 23-24.
[234] See Scheelhaase and Grimme (2007), p. 260.

geous for European airlines.[235] Another aspect was pointed out by Vespermann and Wald who emphasized that non-EU carrier could deploy the most efficient aircraft to European routes and thus reduce emissions under the EU-ETS.[236] Moreover, Albers et al. evaluated the potential emergence of network reconfigurations by non-European NWCs in response to the EU-ETS. They assumed that non-European carriers might be encouraged to redirect traffic flows and reduce emission costs by creating artificial stops in countries adjacent to the EEA such as Switzerland or Turkey. In their analysis they assessed the economic feasibility of artificial stopovers as a strategic cost saving measure for non-European carriers. However, it was found that those measures could potentially lead to superior setbacks, such as longer traveling times and higher airport charges, so that airline network reconfigurations seem to be unlikely.[237]

Besides route network effects, studies often refer to cross-subsidization as a measure which leads to further competitive distortions in international aviation. Cross-subsidization describes the use of revenues generated from flights excluded from the scheme to offset cost increases for flights under the EU-ETS.[238] Wit et al. stated that therefore especially non-EU airlines that operate a large number of flights outside the EEA may perform cross-subsidization in order to limit air fare increases on flights subject to the EU-ETS. As a result, non-EU airlines might be able to strengthen their competitive position on these routes and gain market share.[239] In contrast, Lowe et al. took an opposing view on cross-subsidization in the aviation industry. Their impact assessment was conducted under the assumption of profit maximizing airlines. They noted that cross-subsidization would require non-EU airlines to allocate additional costs emerging from the EU-ETS to non-EU markets. In order to recover these costs, airlines would have to increase fares in the respective markets. This would result in a loss of market share so that overall profits would be adversely impacted. For this reason, Lowe et al. did not expect airlines to engage in cross-subsidization.[240]

As noted earlier, the inclusion of aviation in the EU-ETS triggered hefty political discussions about the legitimacy of the Aviation Directive. Many non-EU countries heavily

[235] See Scheelhaase et al. (2010), p. 23.
[236] See Vespermann and Wald (2011), p. 1074.
[237] See Albers et al. (2009).
[238] See Faber and Brinke (2011), p. 10.
[239] See Wit et al. (2005), p. 132.
[240] See Lowe et al. (2007), chapter 6.

condemned the legal scope of the EU-ETS. As a response to the promising progress on a global solution for emission reduction from aviation, the inclusion of flights operating in and out of the EEA has been temporarily postponed until November 2013. Currently only flights operated within the EEA are subject to the EU-ETS. Therefore, the eventual decision on restoring the original legislation or establishing an international scheme for aviation will have a significant impact on the distorting effects between European and non-European airlines.

4.4 Industry performance and development

4.4.1 Technological advancement

As an industry that has been constantly in a stage of transformation and technological progress, aviation is argued to be technologically mature.[241] Several studies indicate annual average efficiency improvement rates of 1.0% - 1.7% over the last years.[242] Especially rising fuel prices have stimulated demand for more fuel efficient aircraft and initiated the development of technologically enhanced aircraft such as the Boeing 787 Dreamliner and the greatly awaited Airbus A350. In order to further curb global aviation emissions, the International Air Transport Association (IATA) set out a four pillar strategy pursuing improved technology, effective operations, efficient infrastructure, and positive economic measures. With this initiative the IATA aims to achieve carbon neutral growth of the airline industry from 2020.[243] The inclusion of aviation in the EU-ETS adds an additional cost factor to flight operations. Hence, further market reactions improving the industry efficiency can be assumed. In the following, potential technological advancements in aviation instigated by the EU-ETS are discussed.

The literature suggests two different policies to achieve technological progress by distinguishing between technology push- and pull policies. The former includes subsidies to aircraft manufacturers for technology development programs whereas the latter describes the creation of incentives for eco-efficient technologies.[244] In this context, the

---

[241] See Kroo (2004), p. 1.
[242] See Macintosh and Wallace (2009); Wit et al. (2005); Intergovernmental Panel on Climate Change (1999).
[243] See International Air Transport Association (2009).
[244] See Dings et al. (2000), p. 46.

EU-ETS constitutes a hybrid policy pursuing to meet both stimuli. On the one hand, revenues generated through auctioning are intended to be used to support research and development on emission reduction measures in aviation. On the other hand, the imposition of EUAs on aviation emissions is supposed to encourage further technological progress in the industry. [245] Especially under the projected scarcity of EUAs, advancements on more eco-friendly technologies may be increasingly demanded by airlines. However, advanced technologies are not integrated until they become competitive with existing ones.[246] A technical study by Dings et al. suggest several measures, such as high-speed propellers, ultra high bypass engines, new aircraft configurations, and the use of alternative fuel, which could improve fuel efficiency and thus lower carbon emissions in aviation. However, major technological innovations require huge development costs and still face implementation barriers such as slower cruise speed, safety requirements, and environmental trade-offs.[247] Therefore, groundbreaking technological improvements do not constitute short-term solutions but are only achievable in the distant future.[248]

Besides new technology, it has been suggested to reconfigure existing fleets by replacing old aircraft with new low-emitting aircraft to reduce emissions from aviation. In his assessment, Köhler claimed the early retirement of old high-emission aircraft to have the highest emission reduction potential.[249] However, the long service life of airplanes only allows a gradual diffusion of new fuel efficient aircraft in the existing fleets.[250] In this regard, it is estimated that two thirds of all airplanes that will be used in 2030 are already in service. Therefore, fleet renewals cannot be seen as a viable emission mitigating measure in the near future.[251] In addition, the huge capital investments required for new technology imply long time periods to amortize acquisition costs through improved eco-efficiency. Hence, airlines may instead cope with extra costs arising from the EU-ETS.[252] As a more immediate technological measure to reduce emissions, Kar et al. stated

[245] See European Commission (2008).
[246] See Winchester et al. (2011), p. 3.
[247] See Dings et al. (2000).
[248] See Grimme (2010).
[249] See Köhler (2010).
[250] See Grimme (2010), p. 16.
[251] See Royal Commission on Environmental Pollution (2002), p. 34.
[252] See Mendes and Santos (2008), p. 197.

minor modifications such as technology retrofit of winglets and riblets.[253] Yet, it is estimated that investments for these modifications still outweigh the acquisition costs of EUAs.[254]

It can be concluded that radical technological changes in the aviation industry constitute merely a long-term solution to fight climate change. The EU-ETS is neither expected to trigger significant technological changes, such as improved airframe aerodynamics and engine technologies, nor to accelerate fleet renewals by airlines. In particular, high abatement costs in aviation are likely to be an obstacle for CO_2 emission reductions through innovative technology.[255] Instead, an increasing demand for EUAs which will be further strengthened by continuous industry growth is projected.[256]

4.4.2 Operational improvement

Aside from the implementation of enhanced technologies, airlines can achieve emission reductions through improved operational efficiency. Since the EU-ETS requires airlines to take immediate actions to curb emissions and ease the impact on airlines, time aspects are of particular importance for the implementation of mitigation measures. Operational efficiency improvements represent a short-term solution as airlines can often instantly implement changes in current operations.[257] That is why airlines may favor operational measures in order to ease the financial burden of the EU-ETS. Moreover, unlike innovative eco-efficient technologies, operational measures are generally less capital intensive and are therefore a more viable emission mitigation measure to cope with the EU-ETS.

In order to demarcate different actions improving operational efficiency, Wit et al. distinguished between measures at network level and individual flight level. At the network level, airlines can conduct changes in frequencies, destinations and the overall route network configuration, to increase load factors or change flight distances. Efficiency gains at the individual flight level refer to measures such as adopting continuous

[253] See Kar et al. (2009), p. 11.
[254] See Köhler (2010).
[255] See Anger and Köhler (2010).
[256] See Mendes and Santos (2008), p. 204.
[257] See Institute for European Environmental Policy (2006), pp. 12-13.

descent flight path patterns, optimizing flight speeds, and abolishing fuel tankering.[258] Köhler further suggested Air Traffic Management (ATM) improvements and the optimization of taxi times on the air field as effective measures to achieve further emission reductions.[259]

The aviation industry has already experienced a range of efficiency increasing measures. In particular, rising fuel prices have made efficiency improvements vital to stay competitive in the market. As a consequence, the aviation industry has experienced a continuously enhancing operational conduct over the last 40 years which has led to an industry-wide fuel efficiency improvement of 70%.[260] Today, operations in aviation regarding fuel efficiency and aircraft utilization are fairly advanced so that notable performance improvements may be difficult to achieve. Public initiatives that aim for further efficiency gains are already under way like the SESAR program which tries to improve ATM in Europe. Nevertheless, the EU-ETS has put an additional cost factor on aviation emissions. The imposition of EUAs on CO_2 emissions has changed the cost-benefit ratio for investments in fuel efficient measures. Therefore, airlines may be increasingly encouraged to improve operations once previously unprofitable efficiency measures become economically feasible.

4.4.3 Volume measures and modal shift

The EU-ETS is expected to increase the operational costs and to further exacerbate the issue of maintaining economically sound profit margins in the aviation industry. When additional costs cannot be offset by revenues, airlines mostly need to increase air fares to stay profitable and survive in the market. However, a price increase is often associated with declining passenger numbers as a consequence of demand shifts to competitors or through substitution by alternative transportation services. Once operational measures are no longer economically reasonable to compensate for declining demand,

[258] See Wit et al. (2005), pp. 126-127; Fuel tankering describes the storage of additional fuel due to price differentials between airports or operational reasons such as reducing turnaround times.
[259] See Köhler (2010).
[260] See International Air Transport Association (2009).

airlines need to take volume measures such as the reduction of flight frequencies and the discontinuance of unprofitable flight connections.[261]

As explained earlier, key characteristics of business models, such as passenger structure and network configuration, are influential drivers for change in demand in the aviation industry. Low-cost passengers were found to be more sensitive to price. However, despite high demand elasticity, scholars assume LCCs to pass EU-ETS-induced costs fully on to the passenger. They claim that LCCs cannot compensate any further costs due to the fierce competition in the low-cost segment and correspondingly small profit margins. As a result, a severe decline of demand for LCCs is expected.[262] LCCs may have to reduce the number of flights when operational measures do not offset the decreasing number of passengers. In contrast to this presumption, Mendes and Santos emphasized the impact of volume measures on the airline business and the complexity of the decision making process. Volume measures are a drastic intervention in the business operations of an airline. Thus, other factors, such as historical utilization rates, aircraft property costs, and long-term strategy aspects, are generally considered before implementing volume measures.[263] Thus, it is questionably if EU-ETS costs have the magnitude to impose significant reduction in the number of flights.

The impact analysis of the EU-ETS on the industry performance gives rise to another aspect that is associated with the decrease in demand for air transportation. In this context, scholars referred to the modal shift which describes the demand shift to other means of transportation.[264] An increase of air fares as a cause of EUA charges is likely to impact on the demand for air transport and might divert traffic when effective substitutes become economically more attractive. In particular, on short travel distances which are already served by alternative modes, such as high-speed rail and road transportation, airlines might experience increased competition.[265] Furthermore, short-haul flights are generally more fuel intensive due to the large proportion of landing- and take-off phases relative to the overall flight.[266] Assuming that airlines conduct cost allocation for flights according to induced emissions, fares for short-haul flights are more likely to

261 See Anger and Köhler (2010), p. 42.
262 See Wit et al. (2005), p. 132; Oxera (2003).
263 See Mendes and Santos (2008), p. 201.
264 See Wit and Dings (2002), p. 67.
265 See Mendes and Santos (2008), p. 197.
266 See Mendes and Santos (2008), p. 201.

increase.[267] In this context, the IPCC estimated a share of 10% of intra-European air travel to be substitutable by rail transportation.[268]

It is obvious that most of the transportation services in the aviation industry are not exposed to serious competition with substitutes because of the long travel distance and time saving aspects. Yet, there might be some cases in which the competition structure is affected and substitutes gain momentum. In particular, LCCs might be exposed to some modal shifts as they operate predominantly short-haul flights within the EEA as opposed to NWCs that serve many non-substitutable routes.

[267] See Vespermann and Wald (2011), p. 1073.
[268] See Intergovernmental Panel on Climate Change (1999).

5 Analysis results and management implications

The preceding impact analysis showed that the EU-ETS impacts on airlines in several ways. By taking the individual perspective on airlines, the significant impact of the applied EUA allocation method on profitability was emphasized. In particular, the share of EUAs allocated through auctioning was found to have a decisive impact on the overall cost burden for airlines. It was determined that the Aviation Directive deviates from the general allocation rule of the EU-ETS by fixing the share for auctioning at 15% until the end of the third trading period.[269] For this reason, costs of auctioning are generally lower for airlines than for other EU-ETS members. In addition, the large number of freely allocated EUAs might enable airlines to gain windfall profits if opportunity costs are passed on to the passenger. However, the actual impact on airline profitability depends on the cost pass-through rate that can be achieved at a given price elasticity of demand.

It is widely assumed that airlines become net buyers of allowances. The Aviation Directive limits the quantity of EUAs to 95% of the average historical CO_2 emissions from 2004 to 2006.[270] Considering the current level of emissions from aviation, airlines are likely to face allowance scarcity so that additional EUAs have to be acquired on the carbon market. In order to recover EU-ETS costs from the passenger, airlines need to increase air fares. However, the increase of fare levels is strongly influenced by the competition intensity on the respective flight route. The analysis revealed that on monopolistic routes fare increases are often difficult to achieve because of generally high fare levels. Instead, airlines are likely to use revenues to compensate for extra costs. In the more general case of oligopolistic competition on flight routes, the Bertrand and Cournot strategy, as two typically applied pricing strategies, were analyzed. It was found that both strategies would lead to increasing ticket prices in the long-term. Yet, partial compensation of costs might force small airlines that do not have sufficient financial resources to exit some routes. Overall, it was concluded that the profitability of airlines is likely to reduce regardless of the competition intensity. Airlines either use revenues to compensate for EU-ETS costs and thus lower profit margins or are exposed to demand reductions as a reaction to fare increases.

---

[269] See European Commission (2008). art. 3d.
[270] See European Commission (2008), art. 3c.

Furthermore, the analysis addressed issues emerging from the ongoing growth of air traffic. More specifically, the analysis placed its focus on the increasing congestion of hub airports that are centrally located and connect major city pairs.[271] Airlines face capacity constraints at these airports which were found to limit the extent to which costs can be passed through air fares. At congested airports, airlines need to deal with limited slot availability so that passenger demand often exceeds airline capacity. When supply is limited, airlines tend to set fares at the Demand Clearing Price in order to maximize profits so that further fare increases are often not achievable without a severe decline of demand. However, most recent studies do not predict significant fare increases as a cause of the EU-ETS.[272] As mentioned earlier, most EUAs are allocated free of costs to airlines. Also, recent developments on the carbon market have shown a low price for EUAs which has fluctuated around 5 €/t CO_2.[273] Therefore, the profitability of airlines is assumed to be moderately affected by the EU-ETS.

The intra-industry perspective examined the impact of the EU-ETS on the competition between airlines. In the analysis business model peculiarities and hub locations were identified as strong drivers for competitive distortions in the aviation industry. A comparison between LCCs and NWCs revealed significant differences of impact on the competitiveness of airlines. An assessment of the typical network configurations suggested that NWCs would benefit from their hub-and-spoke network. NWCs operate a large number of feeder flights over relatively short distances to accumulate passengers at hub airports and increase the aircraft utilization on long-haul flights. Transit passengers usually pay the overall fare for the combined service, including the feeder service and the connecting flight. Studies found that these passengers are less sensitive to price changes than passengers on short-haul flights. Therefore, NWCs may be able to pass on EU-ETS-induced costs for feeder flights without facing a severe fall in demand. In contrast, LCCs operate point-to-point connections charging passengers for each flight separately. Consequently, the demand for short- and medium-haul flights from NWCs is likely to be less affected than those operated by LCCs after a fare increase. NWCs may achieve an additional competitive advantage because of the diverse passenger structure. Scientific

[271] See Mott McDonald (2006), chapter 7.
[272] See Leggett et al. (2012); Faber and Brinke (2011); Scheelhaase et al. (2010).
[273] See European Energy Exchange (2013a).

studies argue that the elasticity of demand for business-and first class travelers is lower than for passengers travelling economy class. Hence, NWCs may be able to pass EU-ETS costs on to less price sensitive passengers, and thereby mitigate the impact on demand.

An analysis of the applied free allocation rule gave rise to competitive distortions caused by distributional effects. The current benchmarking regime allocates EUAs based on RTK data of airlines. NWCs may benefit from this output factor and gain a competitive advantage over LCCs. Longer travel distances and higher load factors, resulting from belly cargo, were identified as main drivers of this disparity. The continuous growth of the low-cost segment is likely to intensify adverse distributional effects for LCCs. At present, emission allowances are allocated based on fixed RTK data from 2010. The Aviation directive does not foresee any updating of the monitoring year until the next trading period beginning in 2020. The static allocation approach may be particularly challenging for LCCs to prevent a precarious lack of EUAs to cover growth-induced CO_2 emissions.

Another focal issue in the intra-industry competition concerned the geographical scope of the Aviation Directive. EU and non-EU airlines were found to be differently impacted by the EU legislation. The analysis gave strong reasons to assume that EU NWCs are discriminated by the EU-ETS compared to competitors from third countries. Since hub airports of non-EU NWCs are located outside the EEA, the majority of short- and medium-haul flights, that are generally less fuel efficient, are operated outside the European air space and excluded from the EU-ETS. In addition, might use revenues generated from flights outside the EEA to cross-subsidize intercontinental flights to EEA airports. However, recent changes of the geographical scope of the Aviation Directive have led to the exclusion of flights going into and out of the EEA and had therefore a large impact on international aviation. Currently, non-European airlines hardly have to cover emissions from flights with EUAs. However, EU officials are strongly determined to reinforce previous legislation if the ICAO will not be able to reach an agreement on an international solution to curb aviation emissions until the next ICAO General Assembly in November 2013.

The collective industry perspective took a broader view on the aviation industry. In this part, industry-wide measures that might be incentivized through an emission charge and could change the overall industry performance were analyzed. High abatement costs and implementation barriers were identified to have a strong influence on emission mitigation measures. The analysis concluded that the inclusion of aviation in the EU-ETS is likely to increase the need for low emission aircraft; however, considerable emission reductions through radical technological progress are not expected. In aviation, technological innovations face obstacles such as safety requirements and often require tedious implementation processes to become marketable.

Similar to innovative technologies, accelerated fleet renewal to ground high-emitting aircraft is not assumed to provide a short-term solution given the long-service lives of aircraft. Above all, high abatement costs in the capital intensive aviation industry may counter technological mitigation actions to reduce emissions. For this reason, increased operational efficiency seems a more likely reaction from airlines to lower emission levels in the future. Airlines might change flight maneuvering patterns or increase load factors. Yet, current flight operations are often already optimized to lower fuel consumption which may restrict the potential for emission reductions by operational improvements.

The assessment of possible volume measures and the likelihood of modal shifts to other modes of transportation concluded that the EU-ETS is unlikely to cause a significant reduction of the supply of air services. It was assumed that airlines may be forced to reduce the number of flights if operational measures cannot compensate for declining demand. However, the impact of volume measures on vital fields such as the business strategy may prevent airlines from taking significant volume measures. NWCs may for instance still operate strategically relevant feeder flights even though they might have become unprofitable.[274] Furthermore, modal shifts to other modes of transportation are assumed to be marginal due to the lack of effective substitutes for air transport. Nonetheless, short-haul flights that compete with road and rail transportation could experience some impact by substitution.

Figure 7 provides an overview of the main drivers of impact of the EU-ETS on the aviation industry:

[274] See Anger and Köhler (2010), p. 42.

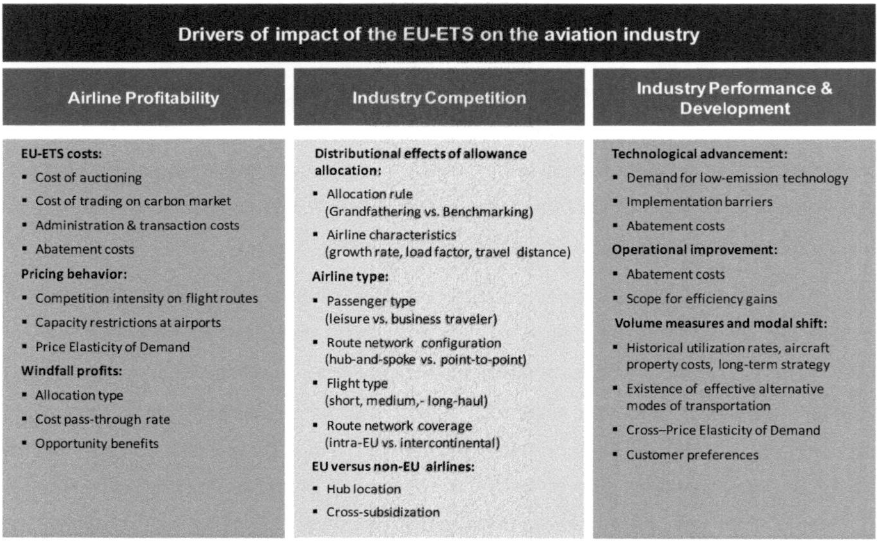

Figure 7: Drivers of impact of the EU-ETS on the aviation industry[275]

The aviation industry is said to be in a technologically mature state. New innovations require long development times until their eventual implementation. The aircraft manufacturer market is in an oligopolistic situation which is dominated by Airbus and Boeing. Hence, it is unlikely that one of them will move forward and take the full investment risk by developing a new aircraft incorporating non-proven technology.[276] In addition, long in-service lifetimes of airplanes prevent airlines from replacing existing fleets. Therefore, radical reductions in emission levels from technological progress are not expected in the near future.[277] In order to reduce CO_2 emissions and mitigate the impact of the EU-ETS, airlines may be well advised to engage in inter-organizational research and development (R&D) projects with aircraft manufacturers to share investment risk. In this way, development projects can be initiated to achieve efficiency improvements through advanced technology and ease the impact of the EU-ETS on aviation.[278]

---

[275] Own illustration.
[276] See Gössling and Upham (2009), p. 299.
[277] See Daley (2010), p. 66.
[278] These projects could be further encouraged through EU subsidies funded by EU-ETS revenues.

Furthermore, a growing interest from airline managers to instigate operational measures to lower CO_2 emissions and mitigate the effect of the EU-ETS is anticipated. Despite all earlier progress on efficiency improvements, there is still potential to achieve further emission reductions. Mendes and Santos state that the improvement of ATM may be the least costly measure to mitigate emissions from aviation.[279] Airline managers may be encouraged to proactively contribute and promote multi-organizational projects, such as the SESAR program, to improve ATM in Europe. The current design of the European air space does not allow for direct routing due to the national sovereignty over air space.[280] Creating a harmonized European air space overcomes this obstacle and allows for shorter flight distances, increasing fuel efficiency, and reduced emissions.[281] Moreover, initiatives related to ATM systems, such as A-CDM, which improves information exchange between stakeholders, including airlines, ATC, airport operators, and ground handlers, could potentially reduce CO_2 emissions.[282] This initiative also counteracts the increasing airport congestion triggered by the constant air traffic growth. Therefore, further emission reductions could be achieved by shortening holding patterns, reducing taxi times, and limiting time delays on runways. According to the IPCC, improvements in ATM whose implementation is anticipated until 2020 could reduce global fuel consumption by 6 to 12%.[283] Besides ATM optimization, a decrease of carrying unusable fuel and the avoidance of fuel tankering constitute further effective operational measures to reduce carbon emissions without considerable investments. Also, improved aircraft maintenance may be a possible measure to limit the impact of the EU-ETS as it ensures high levels of fuel efficiency of airplanes throughout their service lives.[284]

To ease the impact of emission charges on flight operations without decreasing overall emission levels, airlines could reallocation airplanes within their route network. In particular, globally operating NWCs could revise flight network operations and allocate the most fuel efficient aircraft to routes included in the EU-ETS. To achieve further emission reductions, frequencies of feeder flights within the EEA could be decreased by the use of larger aircraft. However, fluctuating passenger numbers at hub airports often

[279] See Mendes and Santos (2008), pp. 196-197.
[280] See Gössling and Upham (2009), p. 301.
[281] See EUROCONTROL (2013b).
[282] See Daley (2010), p. 73.
[283] See Intergovernmental Panel on Climate Change (1999).
[284] See Daley (2010), p. 73.

require high frequencies of feeder services to avoid long travel times so that the feasibility of this measure may be limited.[285] Likewise, significant structural changes regarding network reconfiguration of airlines such as hub relocation are unlikely to occur as Albers et al. suggests.[286] Yet, an increasing number of direct flights instead of widespread hubbing in the EEA could be a conceivable measure to reduce high-emission short-haul flights under the EU-ETS.[287] Also, hub-bypass route planning to reduce the number of flights being dispatched at congested airports could be an alternative to curb emission levels in aviation.[288]

---

[285] See Scheelhaase et al. (2010), p. 24.
[286] See Albers et al. (2009); Hub relocation is more likely for cargo airlines as Derigs and Illing (2013) found out.
[287] See Scheelhaase et al. (2010), p. 24.
[288] See Morrell and Lu (2007).

6 Conclusion and outlook

The inclusion of aviation in the EU-ETS has brought carbon emissions further into focus of decision makers in the industry. Imposing a stringent cap on aviation emissions under continuous air traffic growth has made EUAs an additional factor of production that needs to be considered in future strategic decisions. As it could be seen, the EU-ETS affects the entire aviation industry, including the profitability of airlines, the industry competition, and the overall industry performance and development. The magnitude of impact through the EU-ETS is generally assumed to be rather small compared to other external factors, such as the increase of the oil price, which has causes significant fuel surcharges for airlines. Nonetheless, analyzing individual routes reveals notable differences regarding the impact of the EU-ETS on airlines. Hence, overall changes in strategic behavior and operational practices of market participants can be expected on selected routes. However, abatement costs are generally high in the capital intensive aviation industry and may prevent drastic mission reductions. Moreover, potentially feasible reduction measures in flight operations and technological advances are not assumed to fully offset future CO_2 emissions.[289]

The projected air traffic growth is likely to create EUA scarcity for airlines and trigger increasing demand for EUAs on the carbon market. The carbon price will become a meaningful cost indicator for airline operations in the future. Yet, due to much lower abatement costs in other sectors, the EUA price is not expected to rise significantly. Hence, reductions in aviation emissions are assumed to be modest. In order to create an effective ETS for aviation, it has been suggested to establish a closed trading system. This would lead to a significant increase of the EUA price which would reflect the abatement costs in aviation and therefore encourage airlines to take mitigation measures.[290] Besides an increasing demand for EUAs, investments in emission reduction projects in order to receive international credits are likely to intensify.[291] Therefore, the extent to which international credits can be used to cover CO_2 emissions and the costs of emission reduction projects will probably have a notable impact on the financial burden for airlines.

[289] See Intergovernmental Panel on Climate Change (1999).
[290] See Mendes and Santos (2008), pp. 204-205.
[291] See Faber and Brinke (2011), p. 16.

Above all, the impact on the aviation industry after the inclusion in the EU-ETS will be highly dependent on the development of the future market growth. If air traffic demand is going to continue to rise as in the past, airlines will be under an increasing pressure to engage in emission reduction measures and compensate for growing air traffic. Future actions to stabilize the carbon market, such as a future decrease of the emission cap and a limitation on international credits will have a significant effect on airlines. More importantly, the final decision on the current debate about the establishment of an international ETS for aviation at ICAO level will have existential meaning for the EU-ETS impact on aviation. At present, about two thirds of all aviation emissions originally covered by the Aviation Directive are excluded from the scheme by deferring the enforcement of EU-ETS legislation on intercontinental flights.[292]

Since the imposition of EUAs on CO_2 emissions, climate change has become a major topic in the aviation industry. Managers have to revise their business strategies and need to account for environmental consequences by deciding on operational measures to reduce emissions. However, emission mitigation should not only be seen as a cost reduction measure but also as a chance to improve public reputation. Green technology has been on people's mind for a long time. Also, public interest in the environmental impact of aviation has been popularized like never before. Hence, airlines are well advised to address environmental issues publicly. For instance an airline might publicly promote emission mitigation actions, and thereby communicate awareness of climate change to enhance its market legitimacy. As a result, airlines may built-up a society-wide "green image" which may provide a strategic advantage in the fierce competition of the aviation market.

[292] See Scheelhaase et al. (2010), p. 20.

IV References

Agusdinata, B. and W. de Klein (2002): The dynamics of airline alliances. Journal of Air Transport Management 8(4): 201-211.

Åhman, M., D. Burtraw, J. Kruger and L. Zetterberg (2005): The Ten-Year Rule: Allocation of Emission Allowances in the EU Emission Trading System, discussion paper 05-30: Washington D.C..

Airbus (2012): Global Market Forecast 2012-2031: Toulouse.

Albers, S., J.H. Bühne and H. Peters (2009): Will the EU-ETS instigate new network reconfigurations?. Journal of Transport Management 15(1): 1-6.

Anger, A. (2010): Including aviation in the European emissions trading scheme: Impacts on the industry, CO_2 emissions and macroeconomic activity in the EU. Journal of Transport Management 16(2): 100-105.

Anger, A. and J. Köhler (2010): Including aviation emission in the EU ETS: Much ado about nothing? A review. Transport Policy 17(1): 38-46.

ASEAN (2009): ASEAN Multilateral Agreement on Air Services. 20 May 2009: Manilla.

Auerbach, S. and W. Delfmann (2005): Consolidating the network carrier business model in the European airline industry. In: W. Delfmann, H. Baum, S. Auerbach and S. Albers (eds.): Strategic Management in the Aviation Industry. Ashgate Publishing/Kölner Wissenschaftsverlag: Aldershot, Cologne: 65-97.

Bermig, C. (2005): Competition policy in European aviation markets. In: W. Delfmann, H. Baum, S. Auerbach and S. Albers (eds.): Strategic Management in the Aviation Industry. Ashgate Publishing/Kölner Wissenschaftsverlag: Aldershot, Cologne: 19-41.

Betz, R. and M. Sato (2006): Emission trading: lessons learnt from the 1st phase of the EU ETS and prospects for the 2nd phase. Climate Policy 6(4): 351-359.

Bieger, T. and S. Agosti (2005): Business models in the airline sector – evolution and perspectives. In: W. Delfmann, H. Baum, S. Auerbach and S. Albers (eds.): Strategic Management in the Aviation Industry. Ashgate Publishing/Kölner Wissenschaftsverlag: Aldershot, Cologne: 41-65.

Boeing (2012): Current Market Outlook 2012: Seattle.

Boon, B., M. Davidson, J. Faber and A. van Velzen (2007): Allocation of allowances for aviation in the EU ETS: The impact on the profitability of the aviation sector under high levels of auctioning, final report for World Wide Fund for Nature. CE Delft: Delft.

Brons, M., E. Pels, P. Nijkamp and P. Rietveld (2002): Price elasticities of demand for passenger air travel: a meta-analysis. Journal of Air Transport Management 8(3): 165-175.

Chevallier, J. (2012): Banking and borrowing in the EU ETS: A review of economic modeling, current provisions and prospects for future design. Journal of Economic Surveys 26(1): 157-176.

Chèze, B., J. Chevallier and P. Gastineau (2011): Forecasting world and regional air traffic in the mid-term (2025): An econometric analysis of air traffic determinants using dynamic panel-data models, working paper from Université Paris-Dauphine: Paris.

Competition Commission (2002): A report on the Economic Regulation of the London Airports Companies (Heathrow Ltd, Gatwick Airport Ltd and Stansted Airport Ltd): London.

Court of Justice of the European Union (2011): Reference for a preliminary ruling - Directive 2003/87/EC – Scheme for greenhouse gas emission allowances trading – Directive 2008/101/EC – Inclusion of aviation activities in that scheme – Validity – Chicago Convention – Kyoto Protocol – EU – United States Air Agreement – Principles of customary international law – Legal effects thereof – Whether they may be relied upon – Extraterritoriality of European Union Law – Meaning of charges, fees and taxes. Judgment of Court. Case C-366/10. 21 December 2011: Luxembourg.

Daley, B. (2010): Air Transport and the Environment. Ashgate Publishing: Farnham.

Daraban, B. (2012): The low cost carrier revolution continues: Evidence from the US airline industry. Journal of Business & Economic Research 10(1): 37-44.

Delfmann, W., H. Baum, S. Auerbach and S. Albers (2005): Moving targets: strategic trends in the aviation sector. In: W. Delfmann, H. Baum, S. Auerbach and S. Albers (eds.): Strategic Management in the Aviation Industry. Ashgate Publishing/Kölner Wissenschaftsverlag: Aldershot, Cologne: 1-19.

Derigs, U. and S. Illing (2013): Does EU ETS instigate Air Cargo network reconfiguration? A model-based analysis. European Journal of Operational Research 225(3): 518-527.

De Witt, J. and G. Burghouwt (2008): Slot allocation and the use of hub airports, perspectives for secondary trading. European Journal of Transport and Infrastructure Research 8(2): 147-164.

De Witt Wijnen, R. (2005): Emission Trading under Art. 17 of the Kyoto Protocol. In: D. Freestone and C. Streck (eds.). Legal Aspects of Implementing the Kyoto Protocol Mechanisms: Making Kyoto Work. Oxford: Oxford University Press: 399-411.

Dings J.M.W., P.M. Peeters, J.R. van der Heijden and R.A.A. Winjen (2000): Economic Screening of Aircraft Preventing Emissions. Main Report. Delft.

Doganis, R. (2006): The Airline Business 2nd ed.. Routledge: Abingdon.

Egenhofer, C., M. Alessi, A. Gerorgiev and N. Fujiwara (2011): The EU Emissions Trading System and Climate Policy towards 2050 – Real incentives to reduce emissions and drive innovation?. CEPS Special Report. Brussels.

Ehmer, H., P. Berster, G. Bischoff, W. Grimme, E. Grunewald and S. Maertens (2008): Analyses of the European air transport market – airline business models. Deutsches Zentrum für Luft- und Raumfahrt e.V.. Institute of Air Transport and Airport Research. Cologne.

Elleman, D. and P.L. Joskow (2008): The European Union's Emissions Trading System in Perspective. Arlingtion: The Pew Center on Global Climate Change.

Ernst & Young (2007): Analysis of the EC proposal to include aviation activities in the emission trading scheme (with York Aviation). New York.

EUROCONTROL (2011): Performance Review Report: An assessment of Air Traffic Management in Europe during the calendar year 2010. Brussels.

EUROCONTROL (2013a): Network Management / Airport operations / Airport Collaborative Decision Making. URL: http://www.eurocontrol.int/ (Access 20.02.2013).

EUROCONTROL (2013b): SESAR and Research. URL: http://www.eurocontrol.int/ (Access 06.03.2013).

European Commission (2003): Directive 2003/87/EC of the European Parliament and of the council of 13 October 2003 establishing a scheme for greenhouse gas emission allowance trading within the Community and amending Council Directive 96/61 EC. Official Journal of the European Union L 275: 32-46. Brussels.

European Commission (2004): Directive 2004/101/EC of the European Parliament and of the council of 24 October 2004 amending Directive 2003/87/EC establishing a scheme for greenhouse gas emission allowance trading within the Community, in respect of the Kyoto Protocol's project mechanisms. Official Journal of the European Union L 338: 18-23. Brussles.

European Commission (2005): Communication from the Commission to the Council, the European Parliament, the European Economic and Social committee and the Committee of the Regions – Winning the battle against climate change. COM (2005) 35 final {SEC(2005) 180}. Brussles.

European Commission (2006): Impact Assessment of the inclusion of aviation activities in the scheme for greenhouse gas emission allowance trading within the Community. COM (2006) 818 final {SEC(2006)1685}. Brussels.

European Commission (2008): Directive 2008/101/EC of the European Parliament and of the council of 19 November 2008 amending Directive 2003/87/EC so as to include aviation activities in the greenhouse gas emission allowance trading within the Community. Official Journal of the European Union L 8: 3-21. Brussels.

European Commission (2009a): Directive 2009/29/EC of the European Parliament and of the council of 23 April 2009 amending Directive 2003/87/EC so as to improve and extend the greenhouse gas emission allowance trading scheme of the Community. Official Journal of the European Union L 140: 63-87. Brussles.

European Commission (2009b): EU against climate change – The EU Emissions Trading Scheme. Directorate General for Environment. Luxembourg.

European Commission (2010): Commission Regulation (EU) No 1031/2010 of 12 November 2010 on the timing, administration and other aspects of auctioning of greenhouse gas emission allowances pursuant to Directive 2003/87/EC of the European Parliament and of the Council establishing a scheme for greenhouse gas emission allowances trading within the Community. Official Journal of the European Union L 302: 1-82. Brussels.

European Commission (2011a): Commission Decision of 27 April 2011 determining transnational Union-wide rules for harmonized free allocation of emission allowances pursuant to Art. 10a of Directive 2003/87/EC of the European Parliament and of the Council. Official Journal of the European Union L 130: 1-45. Brussels.

European Commission (2011b): Airport Package – Proposal for a regulation of the European Parliament and the Council on common rules for the allocation of slots at European Union airports. COM (2011) 827 final {SEC 1443, 1444 final}. Brussels.

European Commission (2011c): Joint Procurement Agreement to Procure Common Auction Platforms. 9 November 2011. Brussels.

European Commission (2012a): Proposal for a decision of the European Parliament and the Council amending Directive 2003/87/EC clarifying provisions on the timing of auctions of greenhouse gas allowances. 25 July 2012. Brussels.

European Commission (2012b): Report from the Commission to the European Parliament and the Council – The state of the European carbon market 2012. 14 November 2012. Brussels.

European Commission (2012c): Proposal for a decision of the European Parliament and of the Council derogating temporarily from Directive 2003/87/EC of the European Parliament and of the Council establishing a scheme for greenhouse gas emission allowance trading within the Community. COM (2012) 697. Strasbourg.

European Commission (2013a): Emissions Trading System. URL: http://ec.europa.eu/clima/policies/ets/index_en.htm (Access 18.01.2013).

European Commission (2013b): Emissions Trading System / EU ETS 2005-2012. URL: http://ec.europa.eu/clima/policies/ets/index_en.htm (Access 19.01.2013).

European Commission (2013c): Emissions Trading System / International carbon market. URL: http://ec.europa.eu/clima/policies/ets/index_en.htm (Access 24.01.2013).

European Commission (2013d): Emissions Trading System / Structural reform. URL: http://ec.europa.eu/clima/policies/ets/index_en.htm (Access 20.01.2013).

European Commission (2013e): Australia and European Commission agree on pathway towards fully linking Emission Trading systems. Joint press release. 28 August 2012. Brussels. URL: http://europa.eu/rapid/press-release_IP-12-916_en.htm?locale=en (Access 20.01. 2013).

European Commission (2013f): Stopping the clock of ETS and aviation emissions following last week's International Civil Aviation Organisation (ICAO) Council. MEMO/12/854. Press release. 12 November 2012. Brussels. URL: http://europa.eu/rapid/press-release_MEMO-12-854_en.htm (Access 18.01.2013)

European Commission (2013g): News / Auction of aviation allowances not to resume before June. URL: http://ec.europa.eu/clima/news/index_en.htm (Access 19.04.2013).

European Council (2002a): Council Decision of 25 April 2002 concerning the approval, on behalf of the European Community, of the KP to the United Nations Framework Convention on Climate Change and the joint fulfillment of commitments thereunder (2002/358/CE). Official Journal of the European Communities L 130: 1-20. Luxembourg.

European Council (2002b): Decision No 1600/2002/EC of the European Parliament and the Council of 22 July 2002 laying down the Sixth Community Environment Action Programme. Official Journal of the European Communities L 242: 1-15. Brussels.

European Council (2008): Presidency conclusions of the European Council 11 and 12 December 2008. 13 February 2009. Brussels.

European Energy Exchange (2013a): Market Data / Emission Rights. URL: http://www.eex.com/en/ (Access: 18.02.2013).

European Energy Exchange (2013b): EEX / Products & Fees. URL: http://www.eex.com/en/ (Access: 15.01.2013).

European Environment Agency (2012): Annual European Union greenhouse gas inventory 1990-2010 and inventory report 2012 – Submission to the UNFCCC Secretariat. Technical report No 3/2012. European Environment Agency. 27 May 2012. Copenhagen.

European Low Fares Airline Association (2006): An end to sloppy thinking and hysterical persecution: ELFAA calls for a balanced debate on the environment. Press release. European Low Fares Airline Association. 20 March 2006. Brussels.

European Union (2007): Air Transport Agreement between the United States of America and the European Community. Official Journal of the European Communities L 134: 4-41. 25 May 2007. Brussels.

Faber, J., G. van de Vreede and D.S. Lee (2007): The Impacts of the Use of Different Benchmarking Methodologies on the Initial Allocation of Emission Trading Scheme Permits to Airlines. Final Report to DfT Aviation Environmental Division and the Environment Agency. CE Delft. Delft.

Faber, J. and L. Brinke (2011): The Inclusion of Aviation in the EU Emissions Trading System: An Economic and Environmental Assessment. In: Trade and Sustainable energy Series (5). International Centre for Trade and Sustainable Development. Geneva.

Flenskow, K. (2005): From production-orientation to customer-orientation – modules of a successful airline differentiation strategy. In: W. Delfmann, H. Baum, S. Auerbach and S. Albers (eds.). Strategic Management in the Aviation Industry. Ashgate Publishing/Kölner Wissenschaftsverlag. Aldershot. Cologne: 97-119.

Forsyth, P. (2008): The Impact of Climate Change Policy on Competition in the Air Transport Industry. Discussion paper No. 2008-18. Melbourne.

Freestone, D. (2005): The UN Framework Convention on Climate Change, the Kyoto Protocol and the Kyoto Mechanisms. In: D. Freestone and C. Streck (eds.). Legal Aspects of Implementing the Kyoto Protocol Mechanisms: Making Kyoto Work. Oxford University Press. New York: 3-24.

Frontier Economics (2006): Economic Consideration of extending the EU ETS to include Aviation: A report prepared for the European Low Fares Airline Association (ELFAA). London.

Gillen, D., W.G. Morrison and C. Stewart (2003): Air Travel Demand Elasticities: Concepts, Issues and Measurement. Department of Finance. Canada.

Gillen, D. (2006): Airline Business Models and Networks: Regulation, Competition and Evolution in Aviation Markets. Review of Network Economics 5(4): 366-385.

Gössling, S. and P. Upham (2009): Climate Change and Aviation – Issues, Challenges and Solutions. Earthscan. London.

Goolsbee, A. and C. Syverson (2008): How do incumbants respond to the threat of entry? Evidence from the airline industry. The Quarterly Journal of Economics 123(4): 1611-1633.

Grimme, W. (2010): Measuring the long-term sustainability of air transport – an assessment of the global airline fleet and its CO_2-emissions up to the year 2050. European Transport Conference 2008. Noordwijkerhout.

Grubb, M. (2003): The Economics of the Kyoto Protocol. World Economics 4(3): 143-189.

Hepburn, C., M. Grubb, K. Neuhoff, F. Matthes and M. Tse (2006): Auctioning of EU ETS phase II allowances: how and why?. Climate Policy 6(1): 137-160.

High Court of Justice of England and Wales (2010): Case C-366/10 – The Air Transport Association of America, American Airlines Inc.. Continental Airlines Inc., United Airlines Inc., The Secretary of State for Energy and Climate Change. OJ C 260/9. London.

International Air Transport Association (2009): A global approach to reducing aviation emission – First stop: carbon-neutral growth from 2020.

International Air Transport Association (2011): The economic benefits generated by alliances and joint ventures. IATA Economics Briefing. November 2011. Montreal.

International Civil Aviation Organization (1944): Convention on International Civil Aviation (Doc 7300). Chicago.

International Civil Aviation Organization (2004): Freedoms of the air. Manual on the Regulation of International Air Transportation (Doc 9626. Part 4). Montreal.

International Civil Aviation Organization (2012a): About ICAO / Vision & Mission. URL: http://www.icao.int/Pages/default.aspx (Access 26.11.2012)

International Civil Aviation Organization (2012b): Strategic Objectives / Environmental Protection. URL: http://www.icao.int/Pages/default.aspx (Access 26.11.2012)

International Civil Aviation Organization (2013): Convention on International Civil Aviation signed at Chicago on 7 December 1944. Status of Ratification. URL: http://www.icao.int/secretariat/legal/List%20of%20Parties/Chicago_EN.pdf (Access 19.03.2013)

Institute for European Environmental Policy (2006): Reducing the Impact of Aviation on Climate Change: Economic aspects of the inclusion of the aviation sector in the EU Emission Trading Scheme. Briefing Note (IP/A/ENVI/FWC/2005-35). Study for the European Parliament's Committee on the environment, Public Health and Food Safety by the Institute for European Environmental Policy. Brussels.

Intergovernmental Panel on Climate Change (1999): Aviation and the Global Atmosphere – A Special Report of Working Group I and III of the Intergovernmental Panel on Climate Change. Cambridge University Press. New York.

Intergovernmental Panel on Climate Change (2007): Climate Change 2007 - The Physical Science Basis. Contribution of Working Group I to the Forth Assessment Report of the Intergovernmental Panel on Climate Change. Cambridge University Press. New York.

InterVISTAS (2007): Estimating Air Travel Demand Elasticities. Final Report for IATA. 28 December 2007. Vancouver.

Jäggi, F. (2000): Gestaltungsempfehlungen für Hub-and-Spoke-Netzwerke im Europäischen Luftverkehr : ein ressourcenbasierter Ansatz. PhD Thesis. Universität St. Gallen.

Jegou, I. and L. Rubini (2011): The Allocation of Emission Allowances Free of Charge: Legal and Economic Considerations. In: Transition to a Low Carbon Future Series (18). International Centre for Trade and Sustainable Development. Geneva.

Jepma, C.J. (2003): The EU emission trading scheme (ETS): how linked to JI/CDM?. Climate Policy 3(1): 89-94.

Joint Declaration of the Moscow meeting on inclusion of international civil aviation in the EU-ETS (2012): Adopted by Armenia, Argentina, Republic of Belarus, Brazil, Cameroon, Chile, Cuba, Guatemala, India, Japan, Republic of Korea, Mexico, Nigeria, Paraguay, Russian Federation, Saudi Arabia, Seychelles, Singapore, South Africa, Thailand, Uganda and United States of America. 22 February 2012. Moscow.

Kar, R., P.A. Bonnefoy, R.J. Hansman and S. Sgouridis (2009): Dynamics of Implementation of Mitigating Measures to Reduce Commercial Aviation's Environmental Impacts. Proceedings of the 9th AIAA Aviation Technology, Integration and Operations Conference. 21-23 September 2009. Hilton Head.

Kiehl, J.T. and K.E. Trenberth (1997): Earth's Annual Global Mean Energy Budget. Bulletin of the American Meteorological Society 78(2): 197-208.

Klaas, T. and J. Klein (2005): Strategic airline positioning in the German low cost carrier (LCC) market. In: W. Delfmann, H. Baum, S. Auerbach and S. Albers (eds.). Strategic Management in the Aviation Industry. Ashgate Publishing/Kölner Wissenschaftsverlag. Aldershot. Cologne: 119-143.

Köhler, J. (2010): Air transport: marginal abatement costs and cost reduction through learning. GHG-TransPoRD 3rd workshop. R&D strategies, innovations, learning and cost of measures to reduce greenhouse-gas emissions of transport. December 14-15th 2010. Brussles.

Kokott, J. (2011): Opinion of Advocate General Kokott. Delivered on 6 October 2011. Case-366/10. The Air Transport Association of America and Others. Court of Justice of the European Union. Luxembourg.

Kroo, I. (2004): Innovation in Aeronautics. 42nd AIAA Aerospace Sciences Meeting and Exhibit. 5-8 January 2004. Reno.

Leggett, J.A., D.T. Shedd and B. Elias (2012): Aviation and the European Union Emission Trading Scheme. Report for Congress. Congressional Research Service. Washington, D.C..

Lowe, S., J. Faber, A. Mason, J. Veldhuis, R. Leishout and D. Nelissen (2007): Implications of EU Emission Trading Scheme for Competition Between EU and Non-EU airlines. Draft final report for the Dutch Directorate General for Transport and Civil Aviation (DGTL). In Association with SEO Amsterdam. CE Delft and MVA Consultancy.

Macintosh, A. and L. Wallace (2009): International aviation emissions to 2025: Can emissions be stabilized without restricted demand?. Energy Policy 37(1): 264-273.

MALIAT (2001): Multilateral Agreement on the Liberalization of International Air Transportation. 01 May 2001. Washington D.C..

Malina, R., D. McConnachie, N. Winchester, C. Wollersheim, S. Paltsev and I.A. Waitz (2012): The impact of the European Union Emission Trading Scheme on US aviation. Journal of Air Transport Management 19(1): 36-41.

Mendes, M.Z. and G. Santos (2008): Using economic instruments to address emissions from air transport in the European Union. Environment and Planning A 40(1): 189-209.

Morrell, P. (2007): An evaluation of possible EU air transport emission trading scheme allocation methods. Energy Policy 35(11): 5562-5570.

Morrell, P. and C. Lu (2007): The environmental cost implication of hub-hub versus hub bypass flight networks. Transportation Research Part D (Transport and Environment) 12(3): 143-157.

Morris, J., A. Rowbotham, A. Angus, M. Mann and I. Poll (2009): A Framework for Estimating the Marginal Costs of Environmental Abatement for the Aviation Sector. OMEGA Project 14 – Draft Final Report. Cranfield University. Bedford.

Mott McDonald (2006): Study on the impact of the introduction of secondary trading at Community airports commissioned by the European Commission. November 2006. London.

Neuhoff, K., M. Ahman, R. Betz, J. Cludius, F. Ferrario, K. Holmgren, G. Pal, M. Grubb, F. Matthes, K. Rogge, M. Sato, J. Schleich, J. Sijm, A. Tuerk, C. Kettner and N. Walker (2006): Implications of announced phase II national allocation plans for the EU ETS. Climate Policy 6(4): 411-422.

Oxera (2003): Assessment of the Financial Impact on Airlines of Integration into the EU Greenhouse Gas Emission Trading Scheme. BAA External Emissions Trading Steering Group. Oxford.

PricewaterhouseCoopers (2003): Aviation Emissions and Policy Instruments, Final Report. PricewaterhouseCoopers. 23 September 2005.

Qin, C.Z., C. Stuart (1997): Bertrand versus Cournot revisited. Economic Theory 10(3): 497-507.

Royal Commission on Environmental Pollution (2002): The Environmental Effects of Civil Aircraft in Flight. Special Report. Royal Commission on Environmental Pollution.

Scheelhaase, J.D. and W.G. Grimme (2007): Emissions trading for international aviation – an estimation of the economic impact on selected European airlines. Journal of Air Transport Management 13(5): 253-263.

Scheelhaase, J.D., W.G. Grimme and M. Schaefer (2010): The inclusion of aviation into the EU emission trading scheme – Impacts on competition between European and non-European network airlines. Transportation Research Part D (Transport and Environment) 15(1): 14-25.

Sijm, J.P.M., S.J.A. Bakker, Y. Chen, H.W. Harmsen and W. Lise (2005): CO_2 price dynamics: The implications of EU emission trading for the price of electricity. Petten.

Sijm, J.P.M., K. Neuhoff and Y. Chen (2006): CO_2 cost pass-through and windfall profits in the power sector. Climate Policy 6(1): 49-72.

Tan, K.M. (2011): Incumbent response to entry by low-cost carriers in the U.S. airline industry. Ohio State University Working Paper: 1-33.

Thomson Reuters (2012): Airbus ministers seek delay to EU emission trade scheme. URL: http://www.reuters.com/article/2012/09/11/uk-germany-airshow-emissions-idUSLNE88A02220120911 (Access 03.12.2012).

United Nations (1992): United Nations Framework Convention on Climate Change. 9 May 1992. New York.

United Nations (1997): Kyoto Protocol to the United Nations Framework Convention on Climate Change. Conference of the Parties, third session. FCCC/CP/L.7/Add.1. 1-10 December 1997. Kyoto.

United Nations Climate Change Secretariat (2004): Kyoto Protocol to enter into force 16 February 2005. Press release. 18 November 2004. Bonn.

United Nations Framework Convention on Climate Change (2008): Kyoto Protocol Reference Manual - On accounting of emissions and assigned amount. November 2008. Bonn.

United Nations Framework Convention on Climate Change (2012a): Kyoto Protocol / Status of Ratification of KP. URL: http://unfccc.int/2860.php (Access 29.12.2012).

United Nations Framework Convention on Climate Change (2012b): Essential Background / The Convention / Status of Ratification. URL: http://unfccc.int/2860.php (Access 29.12.2012).

United Nations Framework Convention on Climate Change (2012c): Kyoto Protocol / Doha Amendment. URL: http://unfccc.int/2860.php (Access 29.12.2012.)

United Nations Framework Convention on Climate Change (2012d): Kyoto Protocol / Mechanisms. URL: http://unfccc.int/2860.php (Access 29.12.2012).

United Nations Framework Convention on Climate Change (2013): The Convention. URL: http://unfccc.int/2860.php (Access 05.04.2013).

United States Congress (1978): Airline Deregulation Act of 1978. Public Law 95-504-Oct. 24, 1978. 92 STAT. 1705.

Vespermann J. and A. Wald (2011): Much Ado about Nothing? – An analysis of economic impact and ecologic effects of the EU-emission trading scheme in the aviation industry. Transportation Research Part A 45(10): 1066-1076.

Vivid Economics (2008): A study to estimate the impacts of emissions trading on profits in aviation. A report for Defra and DfT. London.

Winchester, N., C. Wollersheim, R. Clewlow, N.C. Jost, S. Paltsev, J. Reilly and I.A. Waitz (2011): The Impact of Climate Policy on US Aviation. PARTNER Report Series Report No. PARTNER-COE-2011-001. Cambridge.

Windle, R. and M. Dresner (1999): Competitive responses to low cost carrier entry. Transportation Research 35 (1): 59-75.

Wit, R.C.N. and J.M.W. Dings (2002): Economic incentives to mitigate greenhouse gas emissions from air transport in Europe. CE Delft. Delft.

Wit, R.C.N., B. Boon and A. van Velzen (2005): Giving Wings to Emission Trading – Inclusion of Aviation under the European Emission Trading System (ETS): Design and Impacts. Study commissioned by the European Commission & DG Environment. CE Delft. Delft.

Wolf, W. (2007): Verkehr. Umwelt. Klima – Die Globalisierung des Tempowahns. Promedia Verlag. Wien

World Bank (2006): World Development Indicators. April 2006 edition. Washington D.C..

Wråke, M., E. Myers, D. Burtraw, S. Mandell and C. Holt (2010): Opportunity Cost for Free Allocation Emissions Permits: An Experimental Analysis. Environmental and Resource Economics 46(3): 331-336.

V Appendix

Appendix A: Main articles for impact analysis

Document information

Author	Title	Year of Publication
Åhman, M., D. Burtraw, J. Kruger and L. Zetterberg	The Ten-Year Rule: Allocation of Emission Allowances in the EU Emission Trading System	2005

Issues covered

Airline profitability				Industry competition		Industry performance and development		
EU-ETS costs	Pricing behavior	Windfall profits	Distributional effects of allowance allocation	Airline type	European versus non-European airlines	Technological advancement	Operational improvement	Volume measures and modal shift
No	No	No	Yes	No	No	No	No	No

Study characteristics

Research Objective	Research Approach	Key Findings
Development of an efficient and fair allowance allocation approach.	Conceptual essay	In order to ensure fairness and efficiency by applying an allowance allocation method based on historical, a ten-year role for updating the historical emissions is proposed. This period would capture potential gains of companies over time and prevent strategic behavior that would

Document information

Author	Title	Year of Publication
Albers, S., J.H. Bühne and H. Peters	Will the EU-ETS instigate new network reconfigurations?	2009

Issues covered

Airline profitability			Industry competition			Industry performance and development		
EU-ETS costs	Pricing behavior	Windfall profits	Distributional effects of allowance allocation	Airline type	European versus non-European airlines	Technological advancement	Operational improvement	Volume measures and modal shift
No	No	No	No	No	Yes	No	No	No

Study characteristics

Research Objective	Research Approach	Key Findings
To estimate the impact of the EU-ETS on airlines and the likelihood of network configurations.	Using data from OAG to examining selected routes including direct flights into the EEA and flights including stopovers at airports adjacent to the EEA. Operating costs were analyzed by using data from EUROCONTROL's Base of Aircraft Data. The EUA price and demand elasticity was derived from	European hub airlines will be significantly more impacted than non-European carrier due to a larger proportion of flights operated to and from the EEA; Network reconfigurations including artificial stopovers are unlikely due to longer travel times and additional costs such as airport

Document information

Author	Title	Year of Publication
Anger, A. and J. Köhler	Including aviation emission in the EU ETS: Much ado about nothing? A review	2010

Issues covered

Airline profitability			Industry competition			Industry performance and development		
EU-ETS costs	Pricing behavior	Windfall profits	Distributional effects of allowance allocation	Airline type	European versus non-European airlines	Technological advancement	Operational improvement	Volume measures and modal shift
Yes	Yes	No	No	Yes	Yes	No	No	No

Study characteristics

Research Objective	Research Approach	Key Findings
Assessing the economic and environmental impact of the EU-ETS on the aviation industry.	Literature review of EU-ETS impact assessments from 2005-2009.	The overall impact of the EU-ETS on industry growth and CO_2 emissions is relatively small; EU-ETS costs are projected to be passed on to the consumer; Demand for LCC is more elastic than for NWC; Non-EU airlines are proportionally less affected than European airlines due to their

Document information

Author	Title	Year of Publication
Boon, B., M. Davidson, J. Faber and A. van Velzen	Allocation of allowances for aviation in the EU ETS: The impact on the profitability of the aviation sector under high levels auctioning	2007

Issues covered

Airline profitability			Industry competition			Industry performance and development		
EU-ETS costs	Pricing behavior	Windfall profits	Distributional effects of allowance allocation	Airline type	European versus non-European airlines	Technological advancement	Operational improvement	Volume measures and modal shift
No	Yes	Yes	No	No	No	No	No	No

Study characteristics

Research Objective	Research Approach	Key Findings
Assessment of the initial allocation of allowances. In particular, the dependency between the applied allocation method and the cost pass-through rate and the effect on aviation emissions is examined. In addition, the impact of auctioning on airline profitability is evaluated.	The study is conducted by applying the AERO model. Input data were chosen based on different assumptions. Subsequently, a sensitivity analysis was performed by using different scenarios.	In competitive markets where price setting is based on marginal costs, including opportunity costs, costs are fully passed on to the consumer; Under updated benchmarking, opportunity benefits would largely offset the opportunity costs; Airlines will take all measures including technical, operational, and volume measures that cost less than costs for EUAs; Airline profitability is not much affected; If costs cannot be passed through, the operating margin would be adversely

Document information

Author	Title	Year of Publication
Dings J.M.W., P.M. Peeters, J.R. van der Heijden and R.A.A. Winjen	Economic Screening of Aircraft Preventing Emissions	2000

Issues covered

Airline profitability			Industry competition			Industry performance and development		
EU-ETS costs	Pricing behavior	Windfall profits	Distributional effects of allowance allocation	Airline type	European versus non-European airlines	Technological advancement	Operational improvement	Volume measures and modal shift
No	No	No	No	No	No	Yes	No	No

Study characteristics

Research Objective	Research Approach	Key Findings
Are there technologies for reducing aircraft fuel that are: feasible to implement in the long-run or uncompetitive under current market conditions? How much would they cost? Could some technologies enhance environmental efficiency of aircrafts? What are the market barriers for implementation?	The study was conducted by applying the Aircraft Performance (APD) model which calculates aircraft speed, fuel flow, weight, and altitude for about 200 points on the flight path. The Direct Operating Costs (DOC) model was applied to calculate the operating costs of the flight.	It is possible to reduce fuel consumption by 30-40% in the medium term by applying ultra-high bypass turbofan propulsion, and reducing the aircraft's drag and weight; Further reductions could be achieved by implementing propeller propulsion with slowing cruise speed; Direct operating costs could be slightly reduced; Under current market conditions these technological

Document information

Author	Title	Year of Publication
Ernst & Young	Analysis of the EC proposal to include aviation activities in the emission trading scheme	2007

Issues covered

Airline profitability			Industry competition			Industry performance and development		
EU-ETS costs	Pricing behavior	Windfall profits	Distributional effects of allowance allocation	Airline type	European versus non-European airlines	Technological advancement	Operational improvement	Volume measures and modal shift
Yes	Yes	Yes	Yes	Yes	No	No	No	No

Study characteristics

Research Objective	Research Approach	Key Findings
Analyzing the EC impact assessment from 2006.	Theoretical approach which relates to the EC impact assessment from 2006. Objections are supported by various studies and reports.	Airlines have to absorb a large proportion of EU-ETS costs; The cost pass-through rate is influenced by the airline's business model, the exposure to competition, and the position in the market; Demand for air services is highly price sensitive; Due to high demand elasticity and the effects of a liberalized market, windfall profits will not exist in aviation; Airlines will become a net buyer of EUAs due to high abatement costs; The combined costs to cover emissions and auctioning are

Document information

Author	Title	Year of Publication
European Commission	Impact Assessment of the inclusion of aviation activities in the scheme for greenhouse gas emission allowance trading within the Community	2006

Issues covered

Airline profitability			Industry competition			Industry performance and development		
EU-ETS costs	Pricing behavior	Windfall profits	Distributional effects of allowance allocation	Airline type	European versus non-European airlines	Technological advancement	Operational improvement	Volume measures and modal shift
Yes	Yes	Yes	No	Yes	Yes	No	No	No

Study characteristics

Research Objective	Research Approach	Key Findings
Assessing the impact of the EU-ETS on aviation under different policy options.	The impact assessment is conducted by applying three formal models such as AERO, PRIMES, and TREMOVE. The AERO model was used to quantify the economic and environmental impact of possible measures on aviation. The PRIMES model indicates consequences for the energy market induced by EU-ETS measures. TREMOVE projects the potential impact on emissions from the	The inclusion of all flights arriving at and departing from the EU will have the largest environmental impact; Auctioning will only have a small effect on airline profitability as airlines will pass all costs (including opportunity costs) on to the consumer; The impact on air fares will be relatively small; There will be no competitive distortions between airlines regardless of the geographical scope of the

Document information

Author	Title	Year of Publication
Faber, J. and L. Brinke	Inclusion of Aviation in the EU Emissions Trading System: An Economic and Environmental Assessment	2011

Issues covered

Airline profitability			Industry competition			Industry performance and development		
EU-ETS costs	Pricing behavior	Windfall profits	Distributional effects of allowance allocation	Airline type	European versus non-European airlines	Technological advancement	Operational improvement	Volume measures and modal shift
No	No	No	No	No	Yes	No	No	No

Study characteristics

Research Objective	Research Approach	Key Findings
Assessing the economic and environmental consequences of the inclusion of aviation in the EU-ETS.	Conceptual essay	The EU-ETS will have a small impact on ticket prices and demand for air services; Due to high abatement costs, airlines will become net buyers of EUAs and significant emission reductions from aviation are not expected; Some carbon leakage is likely to occur; Cross-subsidization by non-European airlines is unlikely; Transfers at EU-hubs are expected to decrease as well as the number of

Document information

Author	Title	Year of Publication
Faber, J., G. van de Vreede and D.S. Lee	The Impacts of the Use of Different Benchmarking Methodologies on the Initial Allocation of Emission Trading Scheme Permits to Airlines	2007

Issues covered

Airline profitability			Industry competition			Industry performance and development		
EU-ETS costs	Pricing behavior	Windfall profits	Distributional effects of allowance allocation	Airline type	European versus non-European airlines	Technological advancement	Operational improvement	Volume measures and modal shift
No	No	No	Yes	No	No	No	No	No

Study characteristics

Research Objective	Research Approach	Key Findings
Examine the implications of different allocation methods regarding economic efficiency, environmental effectiveness, and distributional impacts on airlines.	The indicative analysis was conducted by applying a spreadsheet model based on UK data. This model calculated CO_2 emissions for generic airline types and the amount of free allowances received by each airline type. The spreadsheet was fed by two databases. The first contained specific airline type characteristics such as route network, fleet, and seating capacities. The second database provided aircraft-specific emission data by using	NWC are relatively well-off under RTK-based benchmarking because of the large number of long-haul flights that generally have high load factors and high fuel efficiency; Output-based benchmarking is the most effective method since it stimulates airlines to increase environmental efficiency and rewards early action; RTK-based benchmarking has relatively small distributional effects; Input-based benchmarks were found to

Document information

Author	Title	Year of Publication
Forsyth, P.	The Impact of Climate Change Policy on Competition in the Air Transport Industry	2008

Issues covered

Airline profitability			Industry competition			Industry performance and development		
EU-ETS costs	Pricing behavior	Windfall profits	Distributional effects of allowance allocation	Airline type	European versus non-European airlines	Technological advancement	Operational improvement	Volume measures and modal shift
No	Yes	No	No	Yes	Yes	No	No	No

Study characteristics

Research Objective	Research Approach	Key Findings
How will climate change policy impact on competition, prices, and profitability in the air transport industry?	Conceptual essay	Impacts on airlines differ according to the market structure whether routes are competitive, monopolistic or oligopolistic; Time scale effects have a large influence on the cost pass-through rate; Short-term fare increases are not expected; In the long-run airlines are expected to increase fares to recover climate change policy-induced costs and restore profitability; Some airlines may exit the market; At congested airports airlines are

Document information

Author	Title	Year of Publication
Frontier Economics	Economic Consideration of extending the EU ETS to include Aviation	2006

Issues covered

Airline profitability			Industry competition			Industry performance and development		
EU-ETS costs	Pricing behavior	Windfall profits	Distributional effects of allowance allocation	Airline type	European versus non-European airlines	Technological advancement	Operational improvement	Volume measures and modal shift
No	Yes	No	Yes	Yes	No	No	No	No

Study characteristics

Research Objective	Research Approach	Key Findings
Assessment of the economic issues of the inclusion of aviation in the EU-ETS.	Conceptual essay	The impact of the EU-ETS for LCCs is larger than for NWCs because of the more sensitive demand for services of LCCs; Aviation is already incentivized to reduce CO_2 emissions by more influential factors such as fuel prices. Hence, significant emission reductions are not expected; The allowance allocation must not be based on grandfathering as it would discourage future abatement efforts. Instead benchmarking allocation based on RTKs presents the most

Document information

Author	Title	Year of Publication
Lowe, S., J. Faber, A. Mason, J. Veldhuis, R. Leishout and D. Nelissen	Implications of EU Emission Trading Scheme for Competition Between EU and Non-EU airlines	2007

Issues covered

Airline profitability			Industry competition			Industry performance and development		
EU-ETS costs	Pricing behavior	Windfall profits	Distributional effects of allowance allocation	Airline type	European versus non-European airlines	Technological advancement	Operational improvement	Volume measures and modal shift
No	No	No	No	No	Yes	No	No	No

Study characteristics

Research Objective	Research Approach	Key Findings
Assessment of the impact on competition between EU and non-EU carriers after the inclusion of aviation in the EU-ETS.	The study was conducted by two different consultancies (MVA and CE Delft). Input for the joint report was delivered by previous studies of each consultancy as well as from expert opinion.	Costs of the EU-ETS will be passed through in fares; The effect will be larger for indirect flights via EU hubs than for flights via non-EU hubs; Large EU NWC will be more impacted on transfer than originating markets; Carriers that operate fuel-efficient aircraft will strengthen their competitive position; There will be a differential impact between EU and non-EU carriers due to hub location; If non-EU carriers already pursue to maximize profits, there will not be any cross-

Document information

Author	Title	Year of Publication
Malina, R., D. McConnachie, N. Winchester, C. Wollersheim, S. Paltsev and I.A. Waitz	The impact of the European Union Emission Trading Scheme on US aviation	2012

Issues covered

Airline profitability			Industry competition			Industry performance and development		
EU-ETS costs	Pricing behavior	Windfall profits	Distributional effects of allowance allocation	Airline type	European versus non-European airlines	Technological advancement	Operational improvement	Volume measures and modal shift
No	Yes	Yes	No	No	No	No	No	No

Study characteristics

Research Objective	Research Approach	Key Findings
Estimate the impact of the EU-ETS on US airlines from 2012 to 2020.	The study is based on an economy-wide computable general equilibrium (CGE) model with a partial equilibrium model on aviation. The CGE mode is an Emission Prediction and Policy Analysis model which is used to analyze the impact of EU-ETS on fuel prices and GDP. To assess airline response the Aviation Portfolio Management Tool for Economics (APMT-E) is used. To assess the impact, a sensitivity analysis using three scenarios (Full, Expense, and Absorb) is applied and	The EU-ETS will have a relatively small impact on aviation emissions due to high abatement costs; The impact on air traffic will be small; Operating revenues increase when costs are passed on to consumers since the revenue impact of reduced traffic is more than offset by increasing air fares due to inelastic demand; If costs are passed through fully, US airlines will generate windfall gains of about $2.6 billion between 2012 and 2020.

Document information

Author	Title	Year of Publication
Mendes, M.Z. and G. Santos	Using economic instruments to address emissions from air transport in the European Union	2008

Issues covered

Airline profitability			Industry competition			Industry performance and development		
EU-ETS costs	Pricing behavior	Windfall profits	Distributional effects of allowance allocation	Airline type	European versus non-European airlines	Technological advancement	Operational improvement	Volume measures and modal shift
No	Yes	No	No	No	No	Yes	No	No

Study characteristics

Research Objective	Research Approach	Key Findings
How will economic instruments impact on demand for air transport? What impact will they have on aviation emissions?	Conceptual essay	The EU-ETS applying grandfathering or auctioning will not curb emissions; An environmental charge reflecting the estimated overall social costs of CO_2 would reduce the number of leisure trips; There will not be any notable mitigation measures due to the high abatement costs relative to the emission charges; To achieve emission reductions, the air transport sector has to be treated separately in a close system which would drive the price for EUAs closer to abatement costs.

Document information

Author	Title	Year of Publication
Morrell, P.	An evaluation of possible EU air transport emission trading scheme allocation methods	2007

Issues covered

Airline profitability			Industry competition			Industry performance and development		
EU-ETS costs	Pricing behavior	Windfall profits	Distributional effects of allowance allocation	Airline type	European versus non-European airlines	Technological advancement	Operational improvement	Volume measures and modal shift
No	No	No	Yes	Yes	No	No	No	No

Study characteristics

Research Objective	Research Approach	Key Findings
How do the possible allowance allocation methods impact on different airline types?	The study evaluates the impact of different allocation methods such as, grandfathering, auction, and benchmarking for three selected UK airlines representing major airline business models.	The impact on LCCs is greater under all allocation methods; The impact on LCCs will be worse if the baseline period is based on less recent emissions; Grandfathering tends to penalize faster growing airlines and favor NWCs. NWCs are able to absorb EU-ETS-evoked costs for feeder flights in the long-

Document information

Author	Title	Year of Publication
Scheelhaase, J.D. and W.G. Grimme	Emissions trading for international aviation – an estimation of the economic impact on selected European airlines	2007

Issues covered

Airline profitability			Industry competition			Industry performance and development		
EU-ETS costs	Pricing behavior	Windfall profits	Distributional effects of allowance allocation	Airline type	European versus non-European airlines	Technological advancement	Operational improvement	Volume measures and modal shift
No	No	No	No	Yes	Yes	No	No	No

Study characteristics

Research Objective	Research Approach	Key Findings
Conceptualizing options how to include aviation in existing ETSs. Providing an overview of current political discussions. Estimating the impacts on operating costs and transport demand for LCCs, NWCs, and regional airlines. Assessing the impact on intra-EU and worldwide airline competition.	The study compares three options for including aviation in the ETS which differ according to allocation method, EUAs price, price elasticity of demand, and growth rate of emissions. Data for Lufthansa, Ryanair, Condor, and air Dolomiti are compared.	The financial impact of the EU-ETS on airlines is relatively moderate; The financial impact on LCCs and regional airlines is significantly larger than for NWCs; The financial success of LCCs is not likely to be adversely impacted due to above-market average profit margins.

Document information

Author	Title	Year of Publication
Scheelhaase, J.D., W.G. Grimme and M. Schaefer	The inclusion of aviation into the EU emission trading scheme – Impacts on competition between European and non-European network airlines	2010

Issues covered

Airline profitability			Industry competition			Industry performance and development		
EU-ETS costs	Pricing behavior	Windfall profits	Distributional effects of allowance allocation	Airline type	European versus non-European airlines	Technological advancement	Operational improvement	Volume measures and modal shift
No	No	No	No	Yes	Yes	No	No	No

Study characteristics

Research Objective	Research Approach	Key Findings
Provides and overview of current political discussions. Estimating the impact on operating costs, ticket prices, and cargo fares for European and non-European NWCs.	A modeling framework is applied comparing Lufthansa and Continental Airlines. The model-based analysis first calculates fuel consumption and CO_2 emissions. Subsequently, it integrates the applied allocation method. Finally, 2012 emission data for both airlines are estimated to make assumptions about the impact of the EU-ETS.	Non-EU NWC with moderate growth between 2006-2012 will gain a competitive advantage over EU NWC; EU NWC will have a competitive disadvantage because of relatively inefficient short-distance flights under the EU-ETS; Airlines with a higher cargo share will benefit from the allocation method and receive more EUAs; Ticket prices for a one-way long-haul flights are expected

Document information

Author	Title	Year of Publication
Vespermann J. and A. Wald	Much Ado about Nothing? – An analysis of economic impact and ecologic effects of the EU-emission trading scheme in the aviation industry	2011

Issues covered

Airline profitability			Industry competition			Industry performance and development		
EU-ETS costs	Pricing behavior	Windfall profits	Distributional effects of allowance allocation	Airline type	European versus non-European airlines	Technological advancement	Operational improvement	Volume measures and modal shift
No	No	No	No	No	Yes	No	No	No

Study characteristics

Research Objective	Research Approach	Key Findings
Analyzing the economic and ecological impact of the inclusion of aviation in the EU-ETS.	The study is performed by using a simulation model accounting for the current Aviation Directive 209/29/EC. The model is based on selected input and dependant variables and uses indices gathered from publicly available sources. The model generates results for the target values emission costs and emission reductions.	Until 2020, the total financial burden caused by the EU-ETS for aviation will be about 3 billion €; Competition distortions are estimated to be rather low; Aviation is considered to become a net buyer of EUAs which will induce emission reduction s in other sectors; The expected emission growth rate of aviation under the EU-ETS is expected to be 1% lower than without the imposition of EUAs.

Document information

Author	Title	Year of Publication
Vivid Economics	A study to estimate the impacts of emissions trading on profits in aviation	2008

Issues covered

Airline profitability			Industry competition			Industry performance and development		
EU-ETS costs	Pricing behavior	Windfall profits	Distributional effects of allowance allocation	Airline type	European versus non-European airlines	Technological advancement	Operational improvement	Volume measures and modal shift
No	Yes	Yes	No	No	No	No	No	No

Study characteristics

Research Objective	Research Approach	Key Findings
Assessing the possible impact on airline profits under different assumptions.	The study applies the latest economic theory (Cournot model) to construct a model which is populated with market data from the aviation industry. It is also based on data from a companion report by Defra "A study to estimate ticket price changes for aviation in the EU ETS".	Profits are likely to decrease even though air fares increase, if the EU-ETS does not apply free EUA allocation; The impact on industry-wide profits with no free allocation is estimated to range between 20% and 40% of the costs of emissions; Larger airlines are expected to face a bigger

Document information

Author	Title	Year of Publication
Wit, R.C.N., B. Boon and A. van Velzen	Giving Wings to Emission Trading – Inclusion of Aviation under the European Emission Trading System (ETS): Design and Impacts	2005

Issues covered

Airline profitability			Industry competition			Industry performance and development		
EU-ETS costs	Pricing behavior	Windfall profits	Distributional effects of allowance allocation	Airline type	European versus non-European airlines	Technological advancement	Operational improvement	Volume measures and modal shift
Yes	Yes	Yes	No	No	Yes	No	Yes	Yes

Study characteristics

Research Objective	Research Approach	Key Findings
Conceptual development of an amendment of Directive 2003/87/EC to address the full climate change impact of aviation through the-EU ETS.	The study analysis three design options to include aviation in the EU-ETS. The primary focus of the analysis is on potential distortions on competitiveness of airlines and distributional impacts of the proposed design options.	There will be only a moderate impact on ticket prices on aviation under all three design options; Windfall profits can be generated if opportunity cost are fully passed on to the consumer; Competitive distortions between EU- and non-EU airlines are unlikely under all three design options.

Appendix B: Supplementary articles for impact analysis

Supplementary articles for impact analysis										
Author	Title	EU-ETSC	PB	WP	DE	AT	EVNE	TA	OI	VM/MS
Betz, R. and M. Sato (2006)	Emission trading: lessons learnt from the 1st phase of the EU ETS and prospects for the 2nd phase				X					
Grimme, W. (2010)	Measuring the long-term sustainability of air transport – an assessment of the global airline fleet and its CO_2-emissions up to the year 2050							X		
Hepburn, C., M. Grubb, K. Neuhoff, F. Matthes and M. Tse (2006)	Auctioning of EU ETS phase II allowances: how and why?	X			X					
Jegou, I. and L. Rubini (2011)	The Allocation of Emission Allowances Free of Charge				X					
Kar, R., P.A. Bonnefoy, R.J. Hansman and S. Sgouridis (2009)	Dynamics of Implementation of Mitigating Measures to Reduce Commercial Aviation's Environmental Impacts								X	
Köhler, J. (2010)	Air transport: marginal abatement costs and cost reduction through learning							X	X	

Author	Title	EU-ETSC	PB	WP	DE	AT	EVNE	TA	OI	VM/MS
Morris, J., A. Rowbotham, A. Angus, M. Mann and I. Poll (2009)	A Framework for Estimating the Marginal Costs of Environmental Abatement for the Aviation Sector	X								
Oxera (2003)	Assessment of the Financial Impact on Airlines of Integration into the EU Greenhouse Gas Emission Trading Scheme	X	X							X
PricewaterhouseCoopers (2003)	Aviation Emissions and Policy Instruments									X
Royal Commission on Environmental Pollution (2002)	The Environmental Effects of Civil Aircraft in Flight							X		
Winchester, N., C. Wollersheim, R. Clewlow, N.C. Jost, S. Paltsev, J. Reilly and I.A. Waitz (2011)	The Impact of Climate Policy on US Aviation	X						X		
Wit, R.C.N. and J.M.W. Dings (2002)	Economic incentives to mitigate greenhouse gas emissions from air transport in Europe									X
Wråke, M., E. Myers, D. Burtraw, S. Mandell and C. Holt (2010)	Opportunity Cost for Free Allocation Emissions Permits: An Experimental Analysis			X						

EU-ETSC (EU-ETS costs); PB (Pricing behavior); WP (Windfall profits); DE (Distributional effects of allowance allocation); AT (Airline type); EVNE (European versus non-European airlines); TA (Technological advancement); OI (Operational improvement); VM/MS (Volume measures and modal shift)